DICTIONARY OF FAMILIAR QUOTATIONS

D1100227

TOPHI BOOKS

Unit 5A, 202–208 New North Road,
London N1 7BJ, England

Contents

Advice

If you can't help, don't hinder.

UNKNOWN

POLONIUS' ADVICE

Neither a borrower nor a lender be;
For loan oft loses both itself and friend
And borrowing dulls the edge of husbandry.
This above all: to thine own self be true,
And it must follow, as the night the day,
Thou canst not then be false to any man.

WILLIAM SHAKESPEARE

Make yourself an honest man, and then you may be sure that there is one rascal less in the world.

THOMAS CARLYLE

At a great bargain make a pause.

UNKNOWN

Everyone should sweep before his own door.

UNKNOWN

You may be an ardent worker,
  But, no matter what you do,
Always watch the other fellow,
  For he may be working you.
Don't take any undue chances,
  Always to yourself be true;
Work your neighbor on the quiet
  While he's planning to work you.

UNKNOWN

A promise should be given with caution and kept with care.

UNKNOWN

When some great sorrow, like a mighty
    river,
  Flows through your life with peace—
    destroying power,
And dearest things are swept from
    sight forever,
  Say to your heart each trying hour:
  "This, too, shall pass away."

LANTA WILSON SMITH

Give every man thy ear, but few thy voice.

WILLIAM SHAKESPEARE

DIVINE LAW

If you would keep young and happy, be good; live a high moral life; practice the principles of the brotherhood of man; send out good thoughts to all, and think evil of no man. This is in obedience to the great natural law; to live otherwise is to break this great Divine law. Other things being equal, it is the cleanest, purest minds that live long and are happy. The man who is growing and developing intellectually does not grow old like the man who has stopped advancing, but when ambition, aspirations and ideals halt, old age begins.

UNKNOWN

Practice yourself what you preach.

PLAUTUS

Let no man presume to give advice to others that has not first given good counsel to himself.

SENECA

Do not count your chickens before they are hatched.

AESOP

Let no pleasure tempt thee, no profit allure thee, no ambition corrupt thee, to do anything which thou knowest to be evil; so shalt thou always live jollily; for a good conscience is a continual Christmas.

BENJAMIN FRANKLIN

A NEW CHANCE

Finish every day and be done with it. You have done what you could. Some blunders and some absurdities no doubt crept in; forget them as soon as you can. Tomorrow is a new day; begin it well and serenely with too high a spirit to be cumbered with your old nonsense. This day is all that is good and fair. It is too dear, with its hopes and invitations, to waste a moment on the yesterdays.

RALPH WALDO EMERSON

Better be silent than speak ill.

UNKNOWN

Of listening children have your fears, for little pitchers have great ears.

UNKNOWN

Put your shoulder to the wheel.

AESOP

Cut your coat according to your cloth.

UNKNOWN

Waste not, want not.

THOMAS HARDY

Before you run in double harness, look well to the other horse.

UNKNOWN

Confess that you were wrong yesterday; it will show that you are wise today.

UNKNOWN

Be always displeased with what thou art, if thou desirest to attain to what thou art not; for where thou hast pleased thyself, there thou abidest. But if thou sayest I have enough, thou perishest. Always add, always walk, always proceed. Neither stand still, nor go back, nor deviate.

ST. AUGUSTINE

Help yourself, and Heaven will help you.

JEAN DE LA FONTAINE

It is a good thing to learn caution by the misfortunes of others.

PUBLIUS SYRUS

Go to friends for advice;
To women for pity;
To strangers for charity;
To relatives for nothing.

SPANISH PROVERB

If you wish a thing done, go; if not, send.

UNKNOWN

Never promise more than you can perform.

PUBLIUS SYRUS

Be wise,
Soar not too high to fall, but stoop to rise.

PHILIP MASSINGER

He who can take advice is sometimes superior to him who can give it.

KARL VON KNEBEL

Measure not men by Sundays, without re-
garding what they do all the week after.

FULLER

Be neither too early in the fashion, nor
too long out of it; nor at any time in the
extremities of it.

JOHN CASPAR LAVATER

Put yourself in his place!

CHARLES READE

FORTITUDE

Laugh, and the world laughs with you;
Weep, and you weep alone.
For the sad old earth must borrow its mirth,
But has trouble enough of its own.
Sing, and the hills will answer;
Sigh, it is lost on the air.
The echoes bound to a joyful sound,
But shrink from voicing care.

Rejoice, and men will seek you;
Grieve, and they turn and go.
They want full measure of all your pleasure,
But they do not need your woe.
Be glad, and your friends are many;
Be sad, and you lose them all.
There are none to decline your nectared
wine,
But alone you must drink life's gall.

Feast, and your halls are crowded;
Fast, and the world goes by.
Succeed and give, and it helps you live,
But no man can help you die.
There is room in the halls of pleasure
For a long and lordly train,
But one by one we must all file on
Through the narrow aisles of pain.

ELLA WHEELER WILCOX

Waste not fresh tears over old griefs.

EURIPIDES

Go, bury thy sorrow,
  The world hath its share;
Go, bury it deeply,
  Go, hide it with care.
Go, bury thy sorrow,
  Let others be blest;
Go, give them the sunshine,
  And tell God the rest.

UNKNOWN

Keep justice, keep generosity, yielding to neither singly.

MARTIN FARQUHAR TUPPER

REST

Are you very weary? Rest a little bit.
In some quiet corner, fold your hands and
    sit.
Do not let the trials that have grieved you
    all the day
Haunt this quiet corner; drive them all
    away!
Let your heart grow empty of every thought
    unkind
That peace may hover round you, and joy
    may fill your mind.
Count up all your blessings, I'm sure they
    are not few,
That the dear Lord daily just bestows
    on you.
Soon you'll feel so rested, glad you
    stopped a bit,
In this quiet corner, to fold your hands
    and sit.

UNKNOWN

The one theme of Ecclesiastes is moderation. Buddha wrote that the greatest word in any language was equanimity. William Morris said the finest blessing of life was systematic, useful work. St. Paul declared the greatest thing in the world was love. Moderation, Equanimity, Work and Love—let these be your physicians, and you will need no other.

ELBERT HUBBARD

Are you willing to stoop down and consider the needs and the desires of little children; to remember the weakness and loneliness of people who are growing old; to stop asking how much your friends love you, and ask yourself whether you love them enough; to bear in mind the things that those who live in the same house with you really want, without waiting for them to tell you; to trim your lamp so that it will give more light and less smoke, and to carry it in front so that your shadow will fall behind you; to make a grave for your ugly thoughts, and a garden for your kindly feelings, with the gate open?

HENRY VAN DYKE

To none will we sell, to none deny or delay, right or justice.

MAGNA CARTA

YOUR NAME

You got it from your father. 'Twas the best
    he had to give,
And right gladly he bestowed it—it is yours
    the while you live.
You may lose the watch he gave you and
    another you may claim,
But remember, when you're tempted, to be
    careful of his name.

It was fair the day you got it and a worthy
    name to wear.
When he took it from his father, there was

no dishonor there;
Through the years he proudly wore it, to
his father he was true,
And that name was clean and spotless
when he passed it on to you.

Oh, there's much that he has given that he
values not at all.
He has watched you break your playthings
in the days when you were small,
And you've lost the knife he gave you and
you've scattered many a game.
But you'll never hurt your father if you're
careful of his name.

It is yours to wear forever, yours to wear
the while you live,
Yours, perhaps, some distant morning to
another boy to give,
And you'll smile as did your father smile
above the baby there,
If a clean name and a good name you are
giving him to wear.

EDGAR A. GUEST

Let all your things have their place; let each part of your business have its time.

BENJAMIN FRANKLIN

Recompense injury with justice, and recompense kindness with kindness.

CONFUCIUS

Hail the small sweet courtesies of life, for smooth do they make the road of it.

LAWRENCE STERNE

Speak the language of the company you are in; speak it purely, and unlarded with any other.

CHESTERFIELD

He who receives a good turn should never forget it; he who does one should never remember it.

PIERRE CHARRON

Whose house is of glass, must not throw stones at another.

GEORGE HERBERT

Train up a child in the way he should go and walk there yourself once in a while.

JOSH BILLINGS

Of hasty counsel take good heed, for haste is very rarely speed.

UNKNOWN

Be slow of giving advice, ready to do a service.

ITALIAN PROVERB

FROM "DON'T TROUBLE TROUBLE"

Don't you trouble trouble till trouble
    troubles you.
Don't look for trouble; let trouble look
    for you.

MARK GUY PEARSE

TWELVE THINGS TO REMEMBER —

1. The value of time.
2. The success of perseverance.
3. The pleasure of working.
4. The dignity of simplicity.
5. The worth of character.
6. The power of kindness.
7. The influence of example.

13

8. The obligation of duty.
9. The wisdom of economy.
10. The virtue of patience.
11. The improvement of talent.
12. The joy of originating.

MARSHALL FIELD

The best thing to give your enemy is forgiveness; to an opponent, tolerance; to a friend, your heart; to your child, a good example; to a father, deference; to your mother, conduct that will make her proud of you; to yourself, respect; to all men, charity.

LORD BALFOUR

Experience keeps a dear school, but fools will learn in no other, and scarce in that; for it is true, we may give *advice*, but we cannot give *conduct*. Remember this: they that will not be counseled cannot be helped. If you do not hear reason she will rap you over your knuckles.

BENJAMIN FRANKLIN

Nothing is given so profusely as advice.

DUC DE LA ROCHEFOUCAULD

I have ever held it as a maxim, never to do that through another, which it was possible for me to execute myself.

BARON DE MONTESQUIEU

If you need a physician, employ these three—a cheerful mind, rest, and a temperate diet.

UNKNOWN

Welcome the coming, speed the departing guest.

ALEXANDER POPE

This above all: to thine ownself be true.

WILLIAM SHAKESPEARE

Suit the action to the word, the word to the action.

WILLIAM SHAKESPEARE

Set the cart before the horse.

JOHN HEYWOOD

Never look a gift horse in the mouth.

ST. JEROME

Give to him that asketh thee; and from him that would borrow of thee turn not thou away.

MATTHEW

Let another man praise thee, and not thine own mouth.

SOLOMON

We ask advice, but we mean approbation.

CHARLES CALEB COLTON

Dispense with trifles.

WILLIAM SHAKESPEARE

Service is the rent we pay for our room on earth.

UNKNOWN

I am not an Athenian or a Greek, but a citizen of the world.

SOCRATES

All are not hunters that blow the horn.

FRENCH

A little too late, much too late.

GERMAN

How seldom we weigh our neighbor in the same balance with ourselves.

THOMAS a KEMPIS

There is many a slip 'twixt the cup and the lip.

PALLADAS

He who commences many things finishes but few.

UNKNOWN

He who takes the child by the hand takes the mother by the heart.

UNKNOWN

To err is human, to forgive divine.

ALEXANDER POPE

Sink or swim, live or die, survive or perish, I give my hand and my heart to this vote.

DANIEL WEBSTER

Within a stone's throw of it.

MIGUEL DE CERVANTES

If thou hast a loitering servant, send him of thy errand just before his dinner.

FULLER

When you are an anvil, hold you still;
When you are a hammer, strike your fill.

JOHN FLORIO

By hook or crook.

JOHN WYCLIFFE

Emblem of hell, nursery of vice.

TOM BROWN

To rob Peter and pay Paul.

JOHN HEYWOOD

Age

Young men's minds are always change-able, but when an old man is concerned in a matter, he looks both before and after.

HOMER

My salad days,
When I was green in judgement.

WILLIAM SHAKESPEARE

What matter if I stand alone?
I wait with joy the coming years;
My heart shall reap where it has sown,
And garner up its fruit of tears.

JOHN BURROUGHS

Age is a tyrant, who forbids, at the penalty of life, all the pleasures of youth.

DUC DE LA ROCHEFOUCAULD

The seeds of repentance are sown in youth by pleasure, but the harvest is reaped in age by pain.

CHARLES CALEB COLTON

Every man desires to live long; but no man would be old.

JONATHAN SWIFT

Blessed is the generation in which the old listen to the young; and doubly blessed is the generation in which the young listen to the old.

THE TALMUD

Grow old along with me!
The best is yet to be,
The last of life for which the first was made;
Our times are in His hand
Who saith: "A whole I planned—
Youth shows but half; trust God,
see all nor be afraid."

ROBERT BROWNING

AS I GROW OLD

God keep my heart attuned to laughter
When youth is done;
When all the days are gray days, coming
after
The warmth, the sun.
God keep me then from bitterness,
from grieving,
When life seems cold;
God keep me always loving and
believing
As I grow old.

UNKNOWN

Crabbed age and youth
Cannot live together;
Youth is full of pleasure,

Age is full of care;
Youth like summer morn,
Age like winter weather;
Youth like summer brave,
Age like winter bare;
Youth is full of sport,
Age's breath is short;
Youth is nimble, age is lame;
Youth is hot and bold,
Age is weak and cold;
Youth is wild and age is tame,
Age, I do abhor thee;
Youth, I do adore thee;
O, my love, my love is young.
Age, I do defy thee.
O sweet shepherd, hie thee,
For me thinks thou stay'st too long.

WILLIAM SHAKESPEARE

YOUTH

Youth is not a time of life ... it is a state of mind. It is not a matter of ripe cheeks, red lips and supple knees ... it is a temper of the will, a quality of the imagination, a vigor of the emotions ... it is a freshness of the deep springs of life.

Youth means a temperamental predominance of courage over timidity, of the appetite for adventure over love of ease. This often exists in a man of fifty years more than a boy of twenty.

Nobody grows old merely living a number of years, people grow old only by deserting their ideals. Years wrinkle the skin, but to give up enthusiasm wrinkles the soul. Worry, doubt, self-trust, fear and despair ... these are the long, long years that bow the head and turn the growing spirit back to dust.

Whether seventy or sixteen, there is in every being's heart the love of wonder, the

19

sweet amazement of the stars and star-like things and thoughts, the undaunted challenge of events, the unfailing child-like appetite for what next, and the joy and game of life.

You are as young as your faith, as old as your doubt; as young as your self-confidence, as old as your fear; as young as your hope, as old as your despair.

In the central place of your heart there is a wireless station; so long as it receives messages of beauty, hope, cheer, courage, grandeur and power from the earth, from men and from the Infinite, so long are you young.

When the wires are all down and all the central place of your heart is covered with the snows of pessimism and the ice of cynicism, then are you grown old indeed and may God have mercy on your soul.

UNKNOWN

GROWING OLD

The days grow shorter, the nights grow
    longer;
  The headstones thicken along the way;
And life grows sadder, but love grows
    stronger
  For those who walk with us day by day.
The tear comes quicker, the laugh comes
    slower;
  The courage is lesser to do and dare;
And the tide of joy in the heart falls lower,
  And seldom covers the reefs of care.
But all true things in the world seem truer,
  And the better things of earth seem best,
And friends are dearer, as friends are fewer,
  And love is all as our sun dips west.
Then let us clasp hands as we walk
    together,

And let us speak softly in low, sweet
    tone,
For no man knows on the morrow whether
    We two pass on—or but one alone.

ELLA WHEELER WILCOX

A young man idle, an old man needy.

ITALIAN PROVERB

Walter Savage Landor wrote his "Imaginary Conversations," picturing the love of Pericles and Aspasia, at eighty-five. Izaak Walton went a-fishing and wrote fiction about his luck at ninety. Fontenelle was as light-hearted at ninety-eight as at forty; Carnaro enjoyed better health at ninety-five than at thirty, and Sir Isaac Newton at eighty-five was still smoking the pipe that cost him his lady-love. Simon Cameron went to the Bermudas at ninety to investigate the resources of the Islands.

UNKNOWN

For, as I like a young man in whom there is something of the old, so I like an old man in whom there is something of the young; and he who follows this maxim, in body will possibly be an old man, but he will never be an old man in mind.

CICERO

The greatest comfort of any old age, and that which gives me the highest satisfaction, is the pleasing remembrance of the many benefits and friendly offices I have done to others.

CATO

For age is opportunity no less
Than youth itself, though in another dress,

And as the evening twilight fades away
The sky is filled with stars, invisible by day.

HENRY WADSWORTH LONGFELLOW

To be seventy years young is sometimes far more cheerful and hopeful than to be forty years old.

OLIVER WENDELL HOLMES

The constant interchange of those thousand little courtesies which imperceptibly sweeten life has a happy effect upon the features, and spreads a mellow evening charm over the wrinkles of old age.

WASHINGTON IRVING

If wrinkles must be written upon our brows, let them not be written upon the heart. The spirit should not grow old.

JAMES A. GARFIELD

GROWING OLDER

A little more tired at the close of day,
A little less anxious to have our way,
A little less ready to scold and blame,
A little more care for a brother's name;
And so we are nearing the journey's end,
Where time and eternity meet and blend.

A little less care for bonds and gold,
A little more zeal for the days of old;
A broader view and a saner mind,
And a little more love for all mankind;
And so we are faring down the way
That leads to the gates of a better day.

A little more love for the friends of youth,

A little more zeal for established truth,
A little more charity in our views,
A little less thirst for the daily news;
And so we are folding our tents away
And passing in silence at close of day.

A little more leisure to sit and dream,
A little more real the things unseen,
A little nearer to those ahead,
With visions of those long loved and dead;
And so we are going where all must go—
To the place the living may never know.

A little more laughter, a few more tears,
And we shall have told our increasing years.
The book is closed and the prayers are said,
And we are part of the countless dead;
Thrice happy, then, if some soul can say,
"I live because of their help on the way."

B. G. WELLS

When I was young I was amazed at Plutarch's statement that the elder Cato began at the age of eighty to learn Greek. I am amazed no longer. Old age is ready to undertake tasks that youths shirked because they would take too long.

W. SOMERSET MAUGHAM

Bless'd retirement, friend to life's decline.

OLIVER GOLDSMITH

Better is a poor and wise youth than an old and foolish king.

ECCLESIASTES

Beauty

A THING OF BEAUTY

A thing of beauty is a joy forever:
Its loveliness increases; it will never
Pass into nothingness; but still will keep
A bower quiet for us, and a sleep
Full of sweet dreams, and health, and
    quiet breathing.
Therefore, on every morrow, are we
    wreathing
A flowery band to bind us to the earth,
Spite of despondence, of the inhuman
    dearth
Of noble natures, of the gloomy days,
Of all the unhealthy and o'er-darkened
    ways
Made for our searching; yes, in spite of all,
Some shape of beauty moves away the pall
From our dark spirits. Such the sun, the
    moon,
Trees old and young, sprouting a shady
    boon
For simple sheep; and such are daffodils
With the green world they live in; and
    clear rills
That for themselves a cooling covert make
'Gainst the hot season; the mid-forest
    brake, ·
Rich with a sprinkling of fair musk-rose
    blooms:
And such too is the grandeur of the dooms
We have imagined for the mighty dead;
All lovely tales that we have heard or read:
An endless fountain of immortal drink,
Pouring into us from the heaven's brink.
Nor do we merely feel these essences
For one short hour; no, even as the trees
That whisper round a temple become soon
Dear as the temple's self, so does the moon,

The passion poesy, glories infinite,
Haunt us till they become a cheering light
Unto our souls, and bound to us so fast
That, whether there be shine, or gloom
      o'ercast,
They always must be with us, or we die.

JOHN KEATS

Beauty's but skin deep.

JOHN DAVIES OF HEREFORD

I DIED FOR BEAUTY

I died for beauty, but was scarce
Adjusted in the tomb,
When one who died for truth was lain
In an adjoining room.

He questioned softly why I failed?
"For beauty," I replied.
"And I for truth,—the two are one;
We brethren are," he said.

And so, as kinsmen met a night,
We talked between the rooms,
Until the moss had reached our lips,
And covered up our names.

EMILY DICKINSON

Never lose an opportunity of seeing anything that is beautiful, for beauty is God's handwriting—a wayside sacrament. Welcome it in every fair face, in every fair sky, in every flower, and thank God for it as a cup of blessing.

RALPH WALDO EMERSON

The most natural beauty in the world is honesty and moral truth.—For all beauty is truth.—True features make the beauty of the face; true proportions the beauty of architecture; true measures, the beauty of harmony and music.

LORD SHAFTESBURY

The vain beauty cares most for the conquest which employed the whole artillery of her charms.

EDWARD GARRETT

Books

THE LAND OF MAGIC

There's a wonderful land where I go by
    myself
  Without stirring out of my chair;
I just take a book from the library shelf,
  Turn its pages and presto! I'm there.
In that wonderful country of Yesterday,
  Where "to-morrow" is always the now,"
Where the good ship Adventure is spreading
    her sails,
  While the sea-foam breaks white at
    her prow.

Where the desert sands burn in the African
    sun,
  Where the North shivers under the snow;
Over the mountains and valley where
    strange rivers run
  With hardy explorers I go.
I share, too, in the magic of fairies and
    gnomes;
  I have followed the ways of the sea;
I have studied the fish in their watery
    homes,
  And the bird and the ant and the bee.

I have followed the trail of the first
    pioneers

Over prairie and mountain range;
I have lived with their dangers and shared
    in their fears
In a country so new and so strange.
And then—just like magic—I'm high in
    the air
In a glittering aeroplane!
Swooping in bird-flight now here and
    now there—
Up, up through clouds and the rain!

O ship of adventure! your sails are spread
    wide,
As they fill with the winds of the West;
Restless and swaying, you wait for the tide
    To bear you away on your quest.
With you I will sail for a year and a day,
    To the world's most unreachable nooks,
For there's nothing to hinder the traveler's
    way
    Through the wonderful Country of Books.

EDITH D. OSBORNE

There is nothing so costly as ignorance.

HORACE MANN

Of bad books we can never read too little;
of the good, never too much.

ARTHUR SCHOPENHAUER

A good book is the best of friends, the
same today and forever.

MARTIN FARQUHAR TUPPER

Poetry is the eloquence of truth.

CAMPBELL

I believe the poets; it is they
Who utter wisdom from the central deep,
And, listening to the inner flow of things,
Speak to the age out of eternity.

JAMES RUSSELL LOWELL

When others fail him, the wise man looks
To the sure companionship of books.

ANDREW LANG

My books and heart
Shall never part.

NEW ENGLAND PRIMER

'Til pleasant, sure, to see one's name in
    print;
A book's a book, although there's nothing
    in't.

LORD BYRON

None but an author knows an author's cares,
Or fancy's fondness for the child she bears.

WILLIAM COWPER

The world agrees
That he writes well who writes with ease.

MATTHEW PRIOR

You write with ease to show your breeding
But easy writing's curst hard reading.

RICHARD BRINSLEY SHERIDAN

Books are the ever-burning lamps of accumulated wisdom.

GEORGE WILLIAM CURTIS

THE BIBLE

We search the world for truth. We cull
The good, the true, the beautiful
From graven stone and written scroll,
And all old flower-fields of the soul;
And, weary seekers of the best,
We come back laden from our quest,
To find that all the sages said
Is the Book our mothers read.

JOHN GREENLEAF WHITTIER

To be at home in all lands and all ages; to count nature a familiar acquaintance, and art an intimate friend; to gain a standard for the appreciation of other men's work and the criticism of one's own; to carry the keys to the world's library in one's pocket and feel its resources behind one in whatever task he undertakes; to make hosts of friends among the men of one's own age, who are the leaders in all walks of life; to lose one's self in generous enthusiasms, and co-operate with others for common ends; to learn manners from students who are gentlemen and to form character under professors who are Christian—These are the returns of the college for the best four years of one's life.

WILLIAM DeWITT HYDE

Some there are,
By their good works exalted, lofty minds
And meditative, authors of delight
And happiness, which to the end of time
Will live, and spread, and kindle.

WILLIAM WORDSWORTH

'Tis the mind that makes the body rich.

WILLIAM SHAKESPEARE

The school will teach children how to read, but the environment of the home must teach them what to read. The school can teach them how to think, but the home must teach them what to believe.

CHARLES A. WELLS

A book is a garden, an orchard, a storehouse, a party, a company by the way, a counsellor, a multitude of counsellors.

HENRY WARD BEECHER

No man can be called friendless when he has God and the companionship of good books.

ELIZABETH BARRETT BROWNING

It is a duty incumbent upon upright and credible men of all ranks, who have performed anything noble or praiseworthy, to truthfully record, in their own writing, the principal events of their lives.

BENVENUTO CELLINI

If you are poor I will tell you how you can become rich—richer than any millionaire: Learn to love good books. There are treasures in books that all the money of the world cannot buy, but that the poorest laborer can have for nothing.

My heart goes out to all the great, the self-denying and the good—to the builders of homes, to the inventors, to the artists who have filled the world with beauty, to the composers of music, to the soldiers of the right, to the makers of mirth, to honest men, and to all the loving mothers of the race.

ROBERT G. INGERSOLL

There is no Frigate like a Book
To take us Lands away
Nor any Courses like a Page
Of prancing Poetry—
This Travel may the poorest take
Without offense of Toil—
How frugal is the Chariot
That bears the Human soul.

EMILY DICKINSON

When you sell a man a book
You don't sell him just twelve ounces

30

Of paper and ink and glue—
You sell him a whole new life.

GOOD COMPANY

Consider what you have in the smallest chosen library.

A company of the wisest and wittiest men that could be picked out of all civilized countries in a thousand years have set in the best order the results of their learning and wisdom.

The men themselves were hid and inaccessible, solitary, impatient of interruption, fenced by etiquette; but the thought which they did not uncover to their bosom friend is here written out in transparent words to us, the strangers of another age.

RALPH WALDO EMERSON

We should accustom the mind to keep the best company by introducing it only to the best books.

SYDNEY SMITH

Except a living man there is nothing more wonderful than a book! a message to us from the dead—from human souls we never saw, who lived, perhaps, thousands of miles away. And yet these, in those little sheets of paper, speak to us, arouse us, terrify us, teach us, comfort us, open their hearts to us as brothers.

CHARLES KINGSLEY

Painting is silent poetry, and poetry painting that speaks.

PLUTARCH

31

Impossible is a word only to be found in the dictionary of fools.

NAPOLEON I

A good book is the best of friends, the same today and forever.

MARTIN FARQUHAR TUPPER

Read not to contradict and confute, nor to believe and take for granted, nor to find talk and discourse, but to weigh and consider.

FRANCIS BACON

As a man may be eating all day, and for want of digestion is never nourished, so these endless readers may cram themselves in vain with intellectual food.

ISAAC WATTS

To read without reflecting, is like eating without digesting.

EDMUND BURKE

Books are the windows through which the soul looks out.

HENRY WARD BEECHER

Books are the masters who instruct us without rods and ferrules, without hard words and anger, without clothes or money.

RICHARD DE BURY

Books are a guide in youth, and an entertainment for age. They support us under solitude, and keep us from becoming a burden to ourselves. They help us to forget the crossness of men and things, compose our cares and our passions, and lay our disappointments asleep. When we are weary of the living, we may repair to the dead, who have nothing of peevishness, pride, or design in their conversation.

JEREMY COLLIER

I have somewhere seen it observed, that we should make the same use of a book that the bee does of a flower: she steals sweets from it, but does not injure it.

CHARLES CALEB COLTON

Some books are to be tasted, others to be swallowed, and some few to be chewed and digested.

FRANCIS BACON

The two most engaging powers of an author are to make *new* things *familiar*, and *familiar* things *new*.

JOHNSON

Poets are all who love—who feel great truths—
And tell them.

UNKNOWN

Writers of novels and romances in general bring a double loss on their readers, they rob them both of their time and money; representing men, manners, and things, that never have been, nor are likely to be; either confounding or perverting history or truth, inflating the mind, or committing violence upon the understanding.

LADY MONTAGUE

Have you ever rightly considered what the mere ability to read means? That it is the key which admits us to the whole world of thought and fancy and imagination? To the company of saint and sage, of the wisest and the wittiest at their wisest and wittiest moment? That it enables us to see with the keenest of eyes, hear with the finest ears, and listen to the sweetest voices of all time? More than that, it annihilates time and space for us.

JAMES RUSSELL LOWELL

We are reading the first verse of the first chapter of a book whose pages are infinite. . . .

UNKNOWN

Poetry is the grouping of words, phrases, and ideas that have always loved each other but have never gotten into that combination before.

UNKNOWN

Poetry has been to me "its own exceeding great reward"; it has soothed my afflictions; it has multiplied and refined my enjoyments; it has endeared solitude; and it has given me the habit of wishing to discover the good and the beautiful in all that meets and surrounds me.

COLERIDGE

To know the true value of books, and to derive any satisfactory benefit from them, you must first feel the sweet delight of buying them—you must know the preciousness of possession.

JAMES BALDWIN

Books are the legacies that a great genius leaves to mankind, which are delivered down from generation to generation, as presents to the posterity of those who are yet unborn.

JOSEPH ADDISON

Courage

Of the millions of words written about Winston Churchill, Lady Diana Cooper's are among the most revealing. She wrote, "When I said that the best thing he had done was to give the people courage," he answered "I never gave them courage; I was able to focus theirs."

UNKNOWN

I RESOLVE

To strip the soul of all pretense,
To hold each day in reverence,
To keep the head and heart apace,
To make this world a worth-while place,
To share my bread with those in need,
To tolerate a neighbor's creed,
To keep a stride without a strut,
To make a home in manse or hut,
To have the grit to grin at loss,
To master life and be its boss!

UNKNOWN

There are too many people praying for mountains of difficulty to be removed, when what they really need is courage to climb them.

UNKNOWN

I love the man that can smile in trouble, that can gather strength from distress, and grow brave by reflection. 'Tis the business of little minds to shrink, but he whose heart is firm, and whose conscience approves his conduct, will pursue his principles unto death.

THOMAS PAINE

LIFTING AND LEANING

There are two kinds of people on earth
    today;
Just two kinds of people, no more, I say.

Not the sinner and saint, for it is well
    understood,
The good are half bad, and the bad are
    half good.

Not the rich and the poor, for to rate a
    man's wealth,
You must first know the state of his
    conscience and health.

Not the humble and proud, for in life's
    little span,
Who puts on vain airs, is not counted a
    man.

Not the happy and sad, for the swift flying
    years
Bring each man his laughter and each
    man his tears.

No; the two kinds of people on earth I
    mean,
Are the people who lift, and the people
    who lean.

Wherever you go, you will find the earth's
    masses

Are always divided in just these two classes.

And, oddly enough, you will find too,
   I ween,
There's only one lifter to twenty who lean.

In which class are you? Are you easing
   the load
Of overtaxed lifters, who toil down the road?

Or are you a leaner, who lets others share
Your portion of labor, and worry and care?

ELLA WHEELER WILCOX

You cannot run away from a weakness; you must sometime fight it out or perish. And if that be so, why not now, and where you stand?

ROBERT LOUIS STEVENSON

The truly brave are soft of heart and eyes,
And feel for what their duty bids them do.

LORD BYRON

A brave man may fall, but cannot yield.
A brave man may yield to a braver man.
None but the brave deserve the fair.

JOHN DRYDEN

Courage consists not in blindly overlooking danger, but in seeing it, and conquering it.

JEAN PAUL RICHTER

The better part of valor is discretion; in the which better part I have saved my life.

WILLIAM SHAKESPEARE

Cowards die many times before their death,
The valiant never taste of death but once.

WILLIAM SHAKESPEARE

He that loses wealth loses much: But he that loses courage loses all.

MIGUEL DE CERVANTES

I disapprove of what you say, but I will defend to the death your right to say it.

VOLTAIRE

Keep your fears to yourself; share your courage with others.

UNKNOWN

TO THE QUITTER

The world won't care if you quit
And the world won't whine if you fail;
The busy world won't notice it,
No matter how loudly you wail.

Nobody will worry that you
Have relinquished the fight and gone down
For it's only the things that you do
That are worth while and get your renown.

The quitters are quickly forgot;
Of them the world spends little time;
And a few e'er care that you've not
The courage or patience to climb.

So give up and quit in despair,
And take your place back on the shelf;

But don't think the world's going to care:
You are injuring only yourself.

UNKNOWN

It show'd discretion the best part of valor.

BEAUMONT AND FLETCHER

That's a valiant flea that dares eat his breakfast on the lip of a lion.

WILLIAM SHAKESPEARE

FROM APPARENT FAILURE

It's wiser being good than bad;
   It's safer being meek than fierce;
It's fitter being sane than mad.
   My own hope is a sun will pierce
The thickest cloud earth ever stretched;
   That, after Last, returns the First
Though a wide compass round be fetched;
   That what began best can't end worst,
Nor what God blessed once, prove accurst.

ROBERT BROWNING

Child of despair, and suicide my name.

SAVAGE

The truly valiant dare everything but doing anybody an injury.

SIR PHILIP SIDNEY

No man is worth his salt who is not ready at all times to risk his body, to risk his well-being, to risk his life, in a great cause.

THEODORE ROOSEVELT

I only regret that I have but one life to give for my country.

NATHAN HALE

SEEING

They took away what should have been
    my eyes,
(But I remembered Milton's Paradise)
They took away what should have been my
    ears,
(Beethoven came and wiped away my tears)
They took away what should have been
    my tongue,
(But I had talked with God when I was
    young)
He would not let them take away my soul,
Possessing that, I still possess the whole.

HELEN KELLER

COURAGE

Courage is armor
A blind man wears;
The calloused scar
Of outlived despairs;
Courage is Fear
That has said its prayers.

KARLE WILSON BAKER

One man with courage makes a majority.

ANDREW JACKSON

Be not dismayed nor be surprised
    If what you do is criticized.
Mistakes are made, I'll not deny
    But only made by those who try.

UNKNOWN

It is the cause and not the death, that makes the martyr.

NAPOLEON BONAPARTE

A lover forsaken
    A new love may get;
But a neck that's once broken
    Can never be set.

WALSH

My heart was in my mouth.

PETRONIUS

Death

CROSSING THE BAR

Sunset and evening star,
    And one clear call for me,
And may there be no moaning of the bar,
    When I put out to sea.

But such a tide as moving seems asleep,
    Too full for sound and foam,
When that which drew from out the
        boundless deep
    Turns again home.

Twilight and evening bell,
    And after that the lark!
And may there be no sadness of farewell,
    When I embark;

For tho' from out our bourne of time
        and place
    The flood may bear me far,
I hope to see my Pilot face to face
    When I have crossed the bar.

ALFRED, LORD TENNYSON

LEAD, KINDLY LIGHT

Lead, kindly Light, amid the encircling
        gloom,
    Lead thou me on.
The night is dark, and I am far from home—
    Lead thou me on.

41

Keep thou my feet; I do not ask to see
The distant scene—one step enough for me.

I was not ever thus, nor prayed that thou
  Shouldst lead me on;
I loved to choose and see my path; but
  now,
  Lead thou me on.
I loved the garish day, and, spite of fears,
Pride ruled my will; remember not past
   years.

So long thy power hath blest me, sure
  it still
  Will lead me on,
O'er moor and fen, o'er crag and torment,
  till
  The night is gone;
And with the morn those angel faces smile
Which I have loved long since, and lost
  awhile.

JOHN HENRY NEWMAN

ON DEATH

As a fond mother, when the day is o'er
  Leads by the hand her little child to bed,
  Half willing, half reluctant to be led,
  And leave his broken playthings on the
   floor,
Still gazing at them through the open door,
  Nor wholly reassured and comforted
  By promises of others in their stead,
Which, though more splendid, may not
  please him more;
So Nature deals with us, and takes away
  Our playthings one by one, and by the
  hand
  Leads us to rest so gently, that we go
  Scarce knowing if we wish to go or stay,
  Being too full of sleep to understand
  How far the unknown transcends the
  what we know.

HENRY WADSWORTH LONGFELLOW

As men, we are all equal in the presence of death.

PUBLIUS SYRUS

What you leave at your death, let it be without controversy, else the lawyers will be your heirs.

SIR THOMAS OSBORNE

Death's but a path that must be trod,
If man would ever pass to God.

THOMAS PARNELL

The dead make the living dearer.

THOMAS LYNCH

DEATH

Life! I know not what thou art,
But know that thou and I must part;
And when, or how, or where we met
I own to me's a secret yet.

Life! We've been long together,
Through pleasant and through cloudy
        weather;
'Tis hard to part when friends are dear,
Perhaps 'twill cost a sigh, a tear;
  Then steal away, give little warning,
  Choose thine own time;
Say not "Good night"; but in some
        brighter clime
        Bid me "Good morning."

ANNA LETITIA BARBAULD

May he rest in peace.

ANON. LATIN

None can comprehend eternity but the eternal God. Eternity is an ocean, whereof we shall never see the shore; it is a deep, where we can find no bottom; a labyrinth from whence we cannot extricate ourselves and where we shall ever lose the door.

THOMAS BOSTON

Let us endeavor so to live that, when we come to die, even the undertaker will be sorry.

MARK TWAIN

Ay beauteous is the world, and many a joy
Floats through its wide dominion. But,
  alas,
When we would seize the winged good, it
    flies,
And step by step, along the path of life,
Allures our yearning spirits to the grave.

JOHANN WOLFGANG VON GOETHE

The paths of glory lead but to the grave.

THOMAS GRAY

How wonderful is Death
Death and his brother, Sleep!

PERCY BYSSHE SHELLEY

For a dead opportunity there is no resurrection.

UNKNOWN

Sir, Hell is paved with good intentions.

SAMUEL JOHNSON

I saw him now going the way of all flesh.

JOHN WEBSTER

As sure as death.

BEN JONSON

In the jaws of death.

SEIGNEUR DU BARTAS

No one is so old that he cannot live yet another year, nor so young that he cannot die today.

FERNANDO DE ROJAS

*What's gone, and what's past help
should be past grief.*

WILLIAM SHAKESPEARE

If the doctor cures, the sun sees it; but if he kills, the earth hides it.

SCOTCH PROVERB

Excess of grief for the deceased is madness; for it is an injury to the living, and the dead know it not.

XENOPHON

O death, where is thy sting? O grave,
where is thy victory?

THE BIBLE

Whom the God's love dies young.

MENANDER

Let no man fear to die,
we love to sleep all,
And death is but the sounder sleep.

BEAUMONT

Pale Death with impartial tread beats
at the poor man's cottage door and
at the palaces of kings.

HORACE

The man is dead who for the body lives.

EDWARD YOUNG

The wither'd frame, the ruin'd mind,
The wreck by passion left behind;
A shrivell'd scroll, a scatter'd leaf,
Sear'd by the autumn-blast of grief.

LORD BYRON

We are such stuff
As dreams are made on, and our little life
Is rounded with a sleep.

WILLIAM SHAKESPEARE

FOR ONE LATELY BEREFT

Though now you are bereft and ways
seem black,

With emptiness and gloom on every
    hand;
Someday Time's healing touch will lead
    you back,
   And gradually your heart will understand
That what you bore must come to one
    and all,
   And Peace, the clean white flower born
    of pain,
Will slowly, surely, rise from sorrow's pall,
   And happiness will come to you again.

MARGARET E. BRUNER

Fear not that thy life shall come to an end, but rather fear that it shall never have a beginning.

CARDINAL NEWMAN

Evil

I consider your very testy and quarrelsome people in the same light as I do a loaded gun, which may, by accident, go off and kill one.

WILLIAM SHENSTONE

It has been said the meek shall inherit the earth, but we all want the earth nowadays and I know that it is not the meek who get the earth these days.

DR. PATTON

How sharper than a serpent's tooth it is
To have a thankless child.

WILLIAM SHAKESPEARE

A suspicious parent makes an artful child.

HALIBURTON

Our passions are like convulsion fits, which, though they make us stronger for a time, leave us the weaker ever after.

POPE

The world's a wood, in which all lose
*   their way,*
Though by a different path each goes
*   astray.*

BUCKINGHAM

Whatever it is, I fear Greeks even when they bring gifts.

VIRGIL

The judge is condemned when the criminal is absolved.

PUBLIUS SYRUS

Hell is full of good intentions or desires.

ST. BERNARD

Villain, thou know'st no law of God or
*   man;*
No beast so fierce, but knows some
*   touch of pity.*

WILLIAM SHAKESPEARE

Something is rotten in the state of Denmark.

WILLIAM SHAKESPEARE

Wit larded with malice.

WILLIAM SHAKESPEARE

WORDS

Before I knew how cruel
  Just common talk can be,
I thought that words were singing things
  With colors like the sea.

But since I've felt their caustic lash,
  And know how they can sting,
I hold my breath when words go by
  For fear they will not sing.

UNKNOWN

The bigger they come, the harder they fall.

ROBERT FITZSIMMONS

It is hardly possible to suspect another without having in one's self the seeds of the baseness the other is accused of.

LESZINSKI STANISLAUS

You are not worth the dust which the rude wind blows in your face.

WILLIAM SHAKESPEARE

Power tends to corrupt, and absolute power corrupts absolutely.

LORD ACTON

They that know no evil will suspect none.

BEN JONSON

Evil thoughts intrude in an unemployed mind, as naturally as worms are generated in a stagnant pool.

FROM THE LATIN

The evil that men do lives after them;
The good is oft interr'd with their bones.

WILLIAM SHAKESPEARE

He that falls into sin is a man; that grieves at it may be a saint; that boasteth of it is a devil.

FULLER

For evil news rides post, while good news baits.

JOHN MILTON

Vice stings us even in our pleasures, but virtue consoles us even in our pains.

CHARLES CALEB COLTON

Vice is a monster of so frightful mien,
As to be hated needs but to be seen;
Yet seen too oft, familiar with her face,
We first endure, then pity, then embrace.

ALEXANDER POPE

Vice repeated is like the wandering wind;
Blows dust in others' eyes, to spread itself.

WILLIAM SHAKESPEARE

Treason doth never prosper. What's the
reason?

Why, when it prospers, none dare call it
treason.

SIR JOHN HARRINGTON

The seeds of our punishment are sown
at the same time we commit sin.

HERSIOD

THE SEVEN MODERN SINS

Policies without principles
Pleasure without conscience
Wealth without work
Knowledge without character
Industry without morality
Science without humanity
Worship without sacrifice

UNKNOWN

Nothing is new; we walk where others
        went;
There's no vice now but has its precedent.

HERRICK

If ridicule were employed to laugh men
out of vice and folly, it might be of some
use; but it is made use of to laugh men
out of virtue and good sense, by attack-
ing everything solemn and serious.

ADDISON

PROFANITY

It is no mark of a gentleman to swear.
The most worthless and vile, the refuse of

mankind, the drunkard and the prostitute, swear as well as the best dressed and educated gentleman. No particular endowments are requisite to give a finish to the art of cursing. The basest and meanest of mankind swear with as much tact and skill as the most refined; and he that wishes to degrade himself to the very lowest level of pollution and shame should learn to be a common swearer. Any man has talents enough to learn to curse God, and imprecate perdition on himself and his fellow men.

Profane swearing never did any man any good. No man is the richer or wiser or happier for it. It helps no one's education or manners. It commends no one to any society. It is disgusting to the refined, abominable to the good, insulting to those with whom we associate, degrading to the mind, unprofitable, needless, and injurious to society; and wantonly to profane His name, to call His vengeance down, to curse Him, and to involve His vengeance, is perhaps of all offenses the most awful in the sight of God.

MARTIN LUTHER

He who repeats the ill he hears of another is the true slanderer.

UNKNOWN

Evil habits soil a fine dress more than mud; good manners, by their deeds, easily set off a lowly garb.

PLAUTUS

Forbear to judge, for we are sinners all.

WILLIAM SHAKESPEARE

Some of your hurts you have cured,
*   And the sharpest you still have survived,*
But what torments of grief you endured
*   From evils that never arrived!*

RALPH WALDO EMERSON

Don't advertise: tell it to a gossip!

UNKNOWN

When men speak ill of thee, live so as nobody may believe them.

UNKNOWN

Nor do they trust their tongues alone,
But speak a language of their own;
Can read a nod, a shrug, a look,
Far better than a printed book;
Convey a libel in a frown,
And wink a reputation down;
Or, by the tossing of a fan,
Describe the lady and the man.

SWIFT

Talkers are no good doers.

WILLIAM SHAKESPEARE

Pride that dines on vanity sups on contempt.

BENJAMIN FRANKLIN

Who gossips to you will gossip of you.

TURKISH

Swear not at all; neither by heaven; for it is God's throne: nor by the earth; for it is his footstool; neither by Jersualem; for it is the city of the great king. Neither shalt thou swear by thy head, because thou canst not make one hair white or black. But let your communication be yea, yea; nay nay; for whatsoever is more than these cometh of evil.

ST. MATTHEW

There's too much abstract willing,
      purposing,
In this poor world. We talk by aggregates.
And think by systems, and being used to
      face
Our evils in statistics, are inclined
To cap them with unreal remedies.
Drawn out in haste on the other side the slate.

ELIZABETH BARRETT BROWNING

As empty vessels make the loudest sound, so they that have the least wit are the greatest babblers.

PLATO

The bitter clamor of two eager tongues.

WILLIAM SHAPESPEARE

A secret in his mouth,
Is like a wild bird put into a cage;
Whose door no sooner opens, but 'tis out.

BEN JONSON

The flying rumors gather'd as they roll'd
Scarce any tale was sooner heard than told
And all who told it added something new.

And all who heard it made enlargement,
  too,
In every ear it spread, on every tongue
  it grew.

POPE

Long-breath'd, talkers, minion lispers,
Cutting honest throats by whispers.

SCOTT

  Slander—
Whose edge is sharper than the sword.

WILLIAM SHAKESPEARE

A hundred mouths, a hundred tongues,
And throats of brass, inspired with iron
  lungs.

VIRGIL

A lie should be trampled on and extinguished wherever found. I am for fumigating the atmosphere, when I suspect that falsehood, like pestilence, breathes around me.

CARLYLE

He who gambles picks his own pocket.

UNKNOWN

IN ANGER

When I have lost my temper
I have lost my reason too,

I'm never proud of anything
Which angrily I do.

When I have walked in anger
And my cheeks are flaming red
I have always uttered something
That I wish I hadn't said.

In anger I have never done
A kindly deed, or wise,
But many things for which I know
I should apologize.

In looking back across my life
And all I've lost or made,
I can't recall a single time
When fury ever paid.

UNKNOWN

The best throw of the dice is to throw them away.

UNKNOWN

Those who in quarrels interpose
Must often wipe a bloody nose.

JOHN GAY

Gambling is an express train to ruin.

UNKNOWN

A soft answer turneth away wrath, but grievous words stir up anger.

SOLOMON

Gaming is the son of avarice, but the father of despair.

UNKNOWN

Regularity is unity, unity is godlike, only the devil is changeable.

RICHTER

We often boast that we are never bored, but yet we are so conceited that we do not perceive how often we bore others.

DUC DE LA ROCHEFOUCAULD

ANGER

Be ye angry and sin not; let not the sun go down upon your wrath.

EPH. iv. 26.

Sluggish idleness—the nurse of sin.

SPENSER

And he that does one fault at first,
And lies to hide it, makes it two.

ISAAC WATTS

A man has no more right to say an uncivil thing, than to act one; no more right to say a rude thing to another, than to knock him down.

JOHNSON

Men for their sins
Have shaving, too, entail'd upon their chins.

BYRON

To divest one's self of some prejudices, would be like taking off the skin to feel the better.

LORD GREVILLE

He who will not reason, is a bigot; he who cannot, is a fool; and he who dares not, is a slave.

LORD BYRON

Who purposely cheats his friend, would cheat his God.

JOHANN KASPAR LAVATER

Flattery is a sort of bad money, to which our vanity gives currency.

DUC DE LA ROCHEFOUCAULD

It is the guilt, not the scaffold, which constitutes the shame.

PIERRE CORNEILLE

Who by aspersions throw a stone
At the head of others, hit their own.

GEORGE HERBERT

Everything that deceives may be said to enchant.

PLATO

How just is Providence in all its works.
How swift to overtake us in our crimes!

LANSDOWNE

Brimful of learning, see that pedant stride,
Bristling with horrid Greek, and puff'd with
    pride!
A thousand authors he in vain has read,
And with their maxims stuff'd his empty
    head;
And thinks that without Aristotle's rule,
Reason is blind, and common sense a
    fool!

                                          BOILEAU

She has no head, and cannot think; no heart, and cannot feel. When she moves, it is in wrath; when she pauses, it is amid ruin; her prayers are curses—her God is a demon—her communion is death—her vengeance is eternity—her decalogue written in the blood of her victims; and if she stops for a moment in her infernal flight, it is upon a kindred rock, to whet her vulture fang for a more sanguinary desolation.

                              DANIEL O'CONNELL

I shall curse you with book and bell and candle.

                              SIR THOMAS MALLORY

The road to Hades is easy to travel.

                                          BION

A liar should have a good memory.

                                     QUINTILIAN

A habit of sneering, marks the egotist, or the fool, or the knave or all three.

                         JOHANN KASPAR LAVATER

He that will not be merciful to his beast is a beast himself.

THOMAS FULLER

Liars when they speak the truth are not believed.

ARISTOTLE

'Tis one thing to be tempted,
Another thing to fall.

WILLIAM SHAKESPEARE

There's no more mercy in him than there is milk in a male tiger.

WILLIAM SHAKESPEARE

Fear is the tax that conscience pays to guilt.

GEORGE SEWELL

Double, double, toil and trouble.

WILLIAM SHAKESPEARE

Sin has many tools, but a lie is the handle which fits them all.

OLIVER WENDELL HOLMES

Wicked men obey for fear, but the good for love.

ARISTOTLE

Their love
Lies in their purses; and whoso empties
them,
By so much fills their hearts with deadly
hate.

WILLIAM SHAKESPEARE

The most certain sign of being born with great qualities is to be born without envy.

DUC DE LA ROCHEFOUCAULD

He who envies another admits his own inferiority.

FROM THE LATIN

As rust corrupts iron, so envy corrupts man.

ANTISTHENES

It is no disgrace not to be able to do everything; but to undertake, or pretend to do, what you are not made for, is not only shameful, but extremely troublesome and vexatious.

PLUTARCH

What is food to one, is to others bitter poison.

LUCRETIUS

The vile are only vain; the great are proud.

LORD BYRON

Our envy always lasts longer than the happiness of those we envy.

DUC DE LA ROCHEFOUCAULD

When a man is wrong and won't admit it, he always gets angry.

THOMAS CHANDLER HALIBURTON

Oh, what a tangled web we weave,
When first we practice to deceive!

SIR WALTER SCOTT

Hypocrisy is the homage which vice pays to virtue.

DUC DE LA ROCHEFOUCAULD

He who conceals a useful truth is equally guilty with the propagator of an injurious falsehood.

ST. AUGUSTINE

Spite is a little word but it represents as strange a jumble of feelings and compound of discords, as any polysyllable in the language.

DICKENS

Wine is a turncoat; first a friend, and then an enemy.

FIELDING

The best side of a saloon is the outside.

UNKNOWN

Don't make your nose blush for the sins of your mouth.

UNKNOWN

Brings danger, troubles, cares, and sleepless
   nights
To him who wears a regal diadem.

JOHN MILTON

I begin to smell a rat.

MIGUEL DE CERVANTES

If you get the best of whiskey, it will get
the best of you.

UNKNOWN

Drink like a fish—water only.

UNKNOWN

Drink first dims, then darkens, then
deadens, then damns.

UNKNOWN

Drink injures a man externally, internal-
ly and eternally.

UNKNOWN

Fie! what a spendthrift he is of his tongue!

WILLIAM SHAKESPEARE

Bear with evil, and expect good.

UNKNOWN

If you lose your temper don't look for it.

UNKNOWN

The moral law is written on the tablets of eternity. For every false word or unrighteous deed, for cruelty and oppression, for lust or vanity, the price has to be paid at last.

JAMES ANTHONY FROUDE

Let rules be fix'd that may our rage contain,
And punish faults with a proportion'd pain;
And do not flay him, who deserves alone
A whipping for the fault that he has done.

HORACE

He is not worthy of the honeycomb
That shuns the hive because the bees
*   have stings.*

WILLIAM SHAKESPEARE

With every exertion, the best of men can do but a moderate amount of good; but it seems in the power of the most contemptible individual to do incalculable mischief.

WASHINGTON IRVING

He must have a long spoon that must eat with the devil.

WILLIAM SHAKESPEARE

It is human to err, but diabolical to persevere.

UNKNOWN

All that glistens is not gold,
Gilded tombs do worms enfold.

WILLIAM SHAKESPEARE

By taking revenge, a man is but even with his enemy; but in passing over it, he is superior.

FRANCIS BACON

There was a laughing devil in his sneer,
That raised emotions both of rage and fear,
And where his frown of hatred darkly fell,
Hope, withering, fled, and mercy sighed
    farewell.

LORD BYRON

He used to raise a storm in a teapot.

CICERO

The world wants to be deceived.

SEBASTIAN BRANT

Under every stone lurks a politician.

ARISTOPHANES

We should often be ashamed of our very best actions, if the world only saw the motives which caused them.

DUC DE LA ROCHEFOUCAULD

A stone is heavy, and the sand weighty; but a fool's vexation is heavier than them both.

SOLOMON

I cannot tell how the truth may be;
I say the tale as 'twas said to me.

SIR WALTER SCOTT

Nothing so much prevents our being natural as the desire of appearing so.

DUC DE LA ROCHEFOUCAULD

Words have a longer life than deeds.

PINDAR

The tongue the ambassador of the heart.

LYLY

Ducks lay eggs: geese lay wagers.

UNKNOWN

To give the devil his due.

MIGUEL DE CERVANTES

The devil take the hindmost!

BEAUMONT AND FLETCHER

Faith

Just about any dream
  Grows stronger
If you hold on
  A little longer.

MARGO GINA HART

You believe easily that which you hope for earnestly.

TERENCE

IT'S UP TO YOU

You are the fellow who has to decide
  Whether you'll do it or toss it aside,
You are the fellow who makes up your
    mind
  Whether you'll lead or linger behind—

Whether you'll try for the goal that's afar
  Or be contented to stay just where you
    are.
Take it or leave. Here's something to do,
  Just think it over. It's all up to you!

What do you wish? To be known as a
    shirk
  Or known as a good man who's willing
    to work,
Scorned for a loafer or praised by your
    chief
  Rich Man or poor man or beggar or thief?

Eager or earnest or dull through the day,
  Honest or crooked? It's you who must
    say!
You must decide in the face of the test
  Whether you'll shirk it or give your best.

UNKNOWN

For they can conquer who believe they can.

VIRGIL

Faith is to believe what we do not see, and the reward of this faith is to see what we believe.

ST. AUGUSTINE

Faith builds a bridge across the gulf of death.

EDWARD YOUNG

Works without *faith* are like a fish without water, it wants the element it should live in. A building without a basis cannot stand; faith is the foundation, and every good action is as a stone laid.

FELTHAM

Faith lights us through the dark to Deity.

SIR WILLIAM DAVENANT

Faith is the substance of things hoped for, the evidence of things not seen.

HEBREWS xi, I.

Faith is the soul going out of itself for all its wants.

THOMAS BOSTON

When you get into a tight place and everything goes against you, till it seems as though you could not hold on a minute longer, never give up then, for that is just the place and time that the tide will turn.

HARRIET BEECHER STOWE

To believe in immortality is one thing, but it is first needful to believe in life.

ROBERT LOUIS STEVENSON

The people who influence you are people who believe in you.

HENRY DRUMMOND

In faith Columbus found a path across untried waters.

MARTIN FARQUHAR TUPPER

HOPE

Hope springs eternal in the human breast:
Man never is, but always to be blest.

ALEXANDER POPE

The men whom I have seen succeed best in life have always been cheerful and hopeful men, who went about their business with a smile on their faces, and took the changes and chances of this mortal life like men, facing rough and smooth alike as it came.

CHARLES KINGSLEY

HOPE

Keep a brave spirit, and never despair;
Hope brings you messages through the keen
    air—
Good is victorious—God everywhere.

Grand are the battles which you have to
    fight,
Be not downhearted, but valiant for right;
Hope and press forward, your face to the
    light.

UNKNOWN

I steer my bark with Hope ahead and fear astern.

THOMAS JEFFERSON

Hope is like the sun, which, as we journey toward it, casts the shadow of our burden behind us.

SAMUEL SMILES

THE STAR OF HOPE

No, it is not for the rude breath of man to blow out the lamp of hope.

Instead let us hold it high, a guide by day, a pillar of fire by night, to cheer each pilgrim on his way.

For have there not been times, O God, when we peered into the gloom, and the heavens were hung with black, and then when life was well-nigh gone, we saw a light. It was the Star of Hope!

ELBERT HUBBARD

Optimism is the faith that leads to achievement. Nothing can be done without hope.

HELEN KELLER

Hope is the pillar that holds up the world. Hope is the dream of a waking man.

PLINY

He who has health has hope, and he who has hope has everything.

ARABIAN PROVERB

Hope is a waking dream.

ARISTOTLE

Give me liberty or give me death!

PATRICK HENRY

I will tell you, scholar, I have heard a grave divine say, that God has two dwellings, one in heaven, and the other in a meek and thankful heart.

IZAAK WALTON

There is a danger of leaving God out of our Thanksgiving Day. We are making it a holiday rather than a holy day. It is a day for the public recognition of God as the giver of all good. To leave God out of Thanksgiving Day is as absurd as leaving Christ out of Christmas.

UNKNOWN

Gratitude is the fairest blossom which springs from the soul.

BALLOU

There's a wideness in God's mercy like the
    wideness of the sea,
There is kindness in His justice which is
    more than liberty.
For the love of God is broader than the
    measure of man's mind,
And the heart of the Eternal is most
    wonderfully kind.

UNKNOWN

He does not believe that does not live
according to his belief.

UNKNOWN

GRATITUDE

I thank You for these gifts, dear God,
    Upon Thanksgiving Day—
For love and laughter and the faith
    That makes me kneel to pray.

For life that lends me happiness,
    And sleep that gives me rest,
These are the gifts that keep my heart
    Serene within my breast.

Love, laughter, faith and life and sleep,
    We own them, everyone—
They carry us along the road
    That leads from sun to sun.

MARGARET ELIZABETH SANGSTER

Friendship

Independence? We are all dependent on
one another, every soul of us on earth.

GEORGE BERNARD SHAW

And when he is out of sight, quickly also is he out of mind.

THOMAS à KEMPIS

People are lonely because they build walls instead of bridges.

JOSEPH FORT NEWTON

Never join with your friend when he abuses his horse or his wife, unless the one is about to be sold, and the other to be buried.

CHARLES CALEB COLTON

If a man does not make new acquaintances as he advances through life, he will soon find himself left alone. A man, sir, should keep his friendship in constant repair.

SAMUEL JOHNSON

Friendship often ends in love; but love in friendship never.

CHARLES CALEB COLTON

It is better to decide between our enemies than our friends; for one of our friends will most likely become our enemy; but on the other hand, one of your enemies will probably become your friend.

BIAS

Whilst you are prosperous you can number many friends; but when the storm comes you are left alone.

OVID

Choose your friends with care, that you may have choice friends.

UNKNOWN

The friendship of a child is the brightest gem set upon the circlet of Society.

UNKNOWN

A friend in need is a friend indeed.

WILLIAM HAZLITT

The only way to have a friend is to be one.

RALPH WALDO EMERSON

A joke never gains an enemy, but often loses a friend.

UNKNOWN

Friends have all things in common.

PLATO

Have no friends not equal to yourself.

CONFUCIUS

Better alone than in bad company.

UNKNOWN

A companion's words of persuasion are effective.

HOMER

No guest is so welcome in a friend's house that he will not become a nuisance after three days.

PLAUTUS

Friendship is the only thing in the world concerning the usefulness of which all mankind are agreed.

CICERO

He who hath many friends, hath none.

ARISTOTLE

Chide a friend in private and praise him in public.

SOLON

To lose a friend is the greatest of all losses.

PUBLIUS SYRUS

Old friends are best. King James used to call for his old shoes; they were easiest to his feet.

JOHN SELDEN

A friend to everybody is a friend to nobody.

SPANISH PROVERB

If a friend of mine . . . gave a feast, and did not invite me to it, I should not mind a bit . . . But if . . . a friend of mine had a sorrow and refused to allow me to share it, I should feel it most bitterly. If he shut the doors of the house of mourning against me, I would move back again and again and beg to be admitted, so that I might share in what I was entitled to share. If he thought me unworthy, unfit to weep with him, I should feel it as the most poignant humiliation, as the most terrible mode for which disgrace could be inflicted on me . . . he who can look on the loveliness of the world and share its sorrow, and realize something of the wonder of both, is in immediate contact with divine things, and has got as near to God's secret as any one can get.

OSCAR WILDE

THE ARROW AND THE SONG

I shot an arrow into the air,
It fell to earth, I knew not where;
For, so swiftly it flew, the sight
Could not follow it in its flight.

I breathed a song into the air,
It fell to earth, I knew not where;
For who has sight so keen and strong,
That it can follow the flight of song?

Long, long afterward, in an oak
I found the arrow, still unbroke;
And the song, from beginning to end,
I formed again in the heart of a friend.

HENRY WADSWORTH LONGFELLOW

'Tis something to be willing to commend; but
my best praise is that I am your friend.

THOMAS SOUTHERNE

Make new friends, but keep the old;
    Those are silver, these are gold.
New-made friendships, like new wine,
    Age will mellow and refine.
Friendships that have stood the test—
    Time and change—are surely best.
Brow may wrinkle, hair grow gray;
    Friendship never knows decay.
For 'mid old friends, tried and true,
    Once more our youth renew.
But old friends, alas! may die;
    New friends must their place supply.
Cherish friendship in your breast—
    New is good, but old is best;
Make new friends, but keep the old;
    Those are silver, these are gold.

JOSEPH PARRY

Do not keep the alabaster boxes of your love and tenderness sealed up until your friends are dead. Fill their lives with sweetness. Speak approving, cheering words while their ears can hear them and while their hearts can be thrilled by them.

HENRY WARD BEECHER

There is no more lovely, friendly and charming relationship, communion or company than a good marriage.

MARTIN LUTHER

What can I give Him
Poor as I am?
If I were a shepherd,
I would give Him a lamb,
If I were a Wise Man,
I would do my part,—
But what can I give Him,
Give my heart.

CHRISTINA GEORGINA ROSSETTI

But I will wear my heart upon my sleeve.

WILLIAM SHAKESPEARE

Sweets to the sweet: farewell!

WILLIAM SHAKESPEARE

Good

Better a kind fool than a proud wise man.

ENGLISH

That best portion of a good man's life,
His little nameless unremembered acts
Of kindness and of love.

WILLIAM WORDSWORTH

Gently to hear, kindly to judge.

WILLIAM SHAKESPEARE

A recent moralist has affirmed that the human heart is like a jug. No mortal can look into its recesses, and you can only judge of its purity by what comes out of it.

ANON.

The Golden Rule never tarnishes.

UNKNOWN

Moderation is the silken string running through the pearl chain of all virtues.

JOSEPH HALL

Truth needs no flowers of speech.

POPE

PATIENCE

Endeavor to be patient in bearing the defects and infirmities of others, of what sort soever they be; for thou thyself also hast many failings which must be borne with by others.

THOMAS à KEMPIS

Charity begins at home.

TERENCE

As charity covers a multitude of sins before God, so does politeness before men.

EARL OF CHESTERFIELD

Patience is bitter, but its fruit is sweet.

JEAN JACQUES ROUSSEAU

The sages do not consider that making no mistake is a blessing. They believe, rather, that the great virtue of man lies in his ability to correct his mistakes and continually to make a new man of himself.

WANG YANG-MING

Patience is sorrow's slave.

CHURCHILL

There is, however, a limit at which forbearance ceases to be a virtue.

EDMUND BURKE

Make yourself an honest man, and then you may be sure there is one rascal less in the world.

THOMAS CARLYLE

To err is human, to forgive divine.

ALEXANDER POPE

Did it ever strike you that goodness is not merely a beautiful thing, but by far the most beautiful thing in the whole world? So that nothing is to be compared for value with goodness; that riches, honor, power, pleasure, learning, the whole world and all in it, are not worth having in comparison with being good; and the utterly best thing for a man is to be good, even though he were never to be rewarded for it.

CHARLES KINGSLEY

Truth never dies. The ages come and go;
   The mountains wear away; the seas retire;
Destruction lays earth's mighty cities low;
   And empires, states, and dynasties expire;
But caught and handed onward by the wise,
   Truth never dies.

Though unreceived and scoffed at through
      the years;
   Though made the butt of ridicule and jest;
Though held aloft for mockery and jeers,
   Denied by those of transient power
      possessed,
Insulted by the insolence of lies,
   Truth never dies.

UNKNOWN

The English laws punish vice; the Chinese laws do more, they reward virtue.

OLIVER GOLDSMITH

No radiant pearl, which crested fortune wears,
No gem, that twinkling hangs from beauty's
*   ears;*
Not the bright stars, which night's blue arch
*   adorn;*
Nor rising sun, that gilds the vernal morn;
Shine with such lustre as the tear that
*   flows*
Down virtue's manly cheek or other's woe.

CHARLES ROBERT DARWIN

Purity is the femine, truth the masculine of honor.

AUGUST W. HARE

A willing helper does not wait until he is asked.

UNKNOWN

Reform like charity must begin at home — Once well at home, it will radiate outward, irrepressible, into all that we touch and handle, speak and work, ever kindling new light by incalculable contagion, spreading in geometric ratio far and wide, doing only good wherever it spreads, and not evil.

THOMAS CARLYLE

Does a man speak foolishly?—suffer him gladly, for you are wise. Does he speak erroneously?—stop such a man's mouth with sound words that cannot be gainsaid. Does he speak truly?—rejoice in the truth.

OLIVER CROMWELL

There are three parts in truth: first, the inquiry, which is the wooing of it; secondly, the knowledge of it, which is the presence of it; and thirdly, the belief, which is the enjoyment of it.

FRANCIS BACON

Good words cost no more than bad.

UNKNOWN

He who receives a benefit should never forget it; he who bestows should never remember it.

PIERRE CHARRON

I believe the first test of a truly great man is his humility.

JOHN RUSKIN

Honesty's the best policy.

MIGUEL DE CERVANTES

An honest man's word is as good as his bond.

MIGUEL DE CERVANTES

Pride makes us esteem ourselves; vanity makes us desire the esteem of others. It is just to say, as Dean Swift has done, that a man is too proud to be vain.

BLAIR

One good turn deserves another.

PETRONIUS

We will take the good will for the deed.

FRANCOIS RABELAIS

Master, go on, and I will follow thee
To the last gasp, with truth and loyalty.

WILLIAM SHAKESPEARE

A scar nobly got is a good livery of honor.

WILLIAM SHAKESPEARE

TEN GOOD THINGS

There are ten good things for which no man has ever been sorry:
For doing good to all;
For speaking evil of no one;
For hearing before judging;
For thinking before speaking;
For holding an angry tongue;
For being kind to the distressed;
For asking pardon for all wrongs;
For being patient toward everybody;
For stopping the ear to the tale bearer;
For dis-believing the most of the evil reports.

UNKNOWN

OBEDIENCE

The man who would lift others must be lifted himself, and he who would command others must learn to obey.

UNKNOWN

HORSE SENSE

A horse can't pull while kicking.
   This fact I merely mention.
And he can't kick while pulling.
   Which is my chief contention.

Let's imitate the good old horse
   And lead a life that's fitting;
Just pull an honest load, and then
   There'll be no time for kicking.

UNKNOWN

The greatest homage we can pay to truth is to use it.

RALPH WALDO EMERSON

THE FOE WITHIN

None but one can harm you,
None but yourself who are your greatest
   foe;
He that respects himself is safe from
   others:
He wears a coat of mail that none can
   pierce.

HENRY WADSWORTH LONGFELLOW

To thine own self be true.

SHAKESPEARE

Fame is vapor;
Popularity is an accident.
Riches take wings and fly.

Those who cheer you to-day
May curse you and stab you to-morrow.
Then there is only one thing left—
That is: CHARACTER.

HORACE GREELEY

Who steals my purse steals trash; 'tis
*   something, nothing;*
'Twas mine, 'tis his, and has been slave to
*   thousands;*
But he that filches from me my good name
Robs me of that which not enriches him
And makes me poor indeed.

WILLIAM SHAKESPEARE

When two goats met on a bridge which was too narrow to allow either to pass or return, the goat which lay down that the other might walk over it, was a finer gentleman than Lord Chesterfield.

CECIL

To be both a speaker of words and a doer of deeds.

HOMER

Amusements to virtue are like breezes of air to the flame—gentle ones will fan it, but strong ones will put it out.

DAVID THOMAS

Lands mortgag'd may return, and more
*   esteem'd,*
But honesty once pawn'd, is ne'er
*   redeem'd.*

MIDDLETON

There is a wonderful power in honest work to develop latent energies and reveal a man to himself.

ALEXANDER MACLAREN

Truth is God's daughter.

SPANISH PROVERB

The most useful virtue is patience.

JOHN DEWEY

The first ingredient in conversation is truth; the next, good sense; the third, good humor; and the fourth, wit.

SIR WILLIAM TEMPLE

From the crown of his head to the sole of his foot he is all mirth; he has twice or thrice cut Cupid's bowstring, and the little hangman dare not shoot at him: he hath a heart as sound as a bell, and his tongue is the clapper; for what his heart thinks his tongue speaks.

WILLIAM SHAKESPEARE

All is lost save honor.

FRANCIS I OF FRANCE

Men of ill judgment oft ignore the good
That lies within their hands, till they have
     lost it.

SOPHOCLES

Speak the truth and shame the Devil.

FRANCOIS RABELAIS

Remorse is the echo of a lost virtue.

EDWARD GEORGE BULWER-LYTTON

Happiness

By heaven we understand a state of happiness infinite in degree, and endless in duration.

FRANKLIN

The grand essentials to happiness in this life are something to do, something to love; and something to hope for.

JOSEPH ADDISON

'Mid pleasures and palaces though we may
    roam,
Be it ever so humble, there's no place
    like home.

JOHN HOWARD PAYNE

There is a pleasure sure
In being mad which none but madmen
    know.

JOHN DRYDEN

Put this restriction on your pleasures—be cautious that they injure no being that lives.

JOHANN ZIMMERMAN

Enjoy present pleasures in such a way as not to injure future ones.

SENECA

The proof of the pudding is in the eating.

MIGUEL DE CERVANTES

Pleasure is the beginning and the end of living happily.

EPICURUS

Pleasure that comes unlooked for is thrice welcome.

ROGERS

Pleasure, or wrong or rightly understood,
Our greatest evil, or our greatest good.

POPE

A little nonsense now and then,
Is relish'd by the best of men.

ANON.

On with the dance! let joy be unconfined.

LORD BYRON

Variety's the very spice of life,
That gives it all its flavor.

WILLIAM COWPER

Pleasure soon exhausts us and itself also; but endeavor never does.

RICHTER

Choose such pleasures as recreate much and cost little.

FULLER

The most wasted day of all is that on which we have not laughed.

SEBASTIEN R. N. CHAMFORT

FROM "TO A SKYLARK"

We look before and after,
  And pine for what is not;
Our sincerest laughter
  With some pain is fraught;
Our sweetest songs are those that tell of
    saddest thought.

Yet if we could scorn
  Hate and pride and fear;
If we were things born
  Not to shed a tear,
I know not how thy joy we ever should
    come near.

PERCY BYSSHE SHELLEY

The kindest and the happiest pair
Will find occasion to forbear;
And something, every day they live,
To pity, and perhaps forgive.

WILLIAM COWPER

Our happiness in this world depends on the affections we are enabled to inspire.

DUCHESSE DE PRASLIN

CONTENTMENT

Banish the future; live only for the hour and its allotted work. Think not of the amount to be accomplished, the difficulties to be overcome, but set earnestly at the little task at your elbow, letting that be sufficient for the day; for surely our plain duty is "not to see what lies dimly at a distance, but to do what lies clearly at hand."

SIR WILLIAM OSLER

HAPPINESS

Happiness is a sunbeam which may pass through a thousand bosoms without losing a particle of its original ray; nay, when it strikes a kindred heart, like the converged light on a mirror, it reflects itself with redoubled brightness. It is not perfected till it is shared.

JANE PORTER

There is this difference between happiness and wisdom, that he that thinks himself the happiest man, really is so; but he that thinks himself the wisest, is generally the greatest fool.

CHARLES CALEB COLTON

The happiness of a man in this life does not consist in the absence but in the mastery of his passions.

ALFRED, LORD TENNYSON

East or west, home is best.

UNKNOWN

All who joy would win
Must share it—happiness was born a twin.

LORD BYRON

Laugh yourself into stitches.

WILLIAM SHAKESPEARE

Surely happiness is reflective like the light of heaven; and every countenance, bright with smiles and glowing with innocent enjoyment, is a mirror, transmitting to others the rays of a supreme and ever-shining benevolence.

WASHINGTON IRVING

Some there are,
By their good works exalted, lofty minds
And meditative, authors of delight
And happiness, which to the end of time
Will live, and spread, and kindle.

WILLIAM WORDSWORTH

Rest is the sweet sauce of labor.

PLUTARCH

Happiness is in the taste, and not in the things themselves; we are happy from possessing what we like, not from possessing what others like.

DUC DE LA ROCHEFOUCAULD

Tea! thou soft, thou sober sage, and venerable liquid:—thou female tongue-running, smile-smoothing, heart-opening, wink-tippling cordial, to whose glorious insipidity I owe the happiest moments of my life, let me fall prostrate!

COLLEY CIBBER

Perfect happiness, I believe, was never intended by the Deity to be the lot of one of His creatures in this world; but that He has very much put in our power the nearness of our approaches to it, is what I have steadfastly believed.

THOMAS JEFFERSON

Happy the man, and happy he alone,
  He who can call today his own;
  He who, secure within, can say,
Tomorrow, do thy worst, for I have lived
  today.

JOHN DRYDEN

He has enough who is content.

UNKNOWN

Happiness is unrepented pleasure.

SOCRATES

Contentment is the philosopher's stone, which turns all it toucheth into gold; the poor man is rich with it and the rich man is poor without it.

UNKNOWN

ALTERNATIVES

Not what we have, but what we use;
Not what we see, but what we choose—
These are the things that mar or bless
The sum of human happiness.

UNKNOWN

Happiness grows at our own firesides, and is not to be picked in stranger's gardens.

UNKNOWN

Happiness is a perfume you cannot pour on others without getting a few drops on yourself.

UNKNOWN

Happiness is as a butterfly, which, when pursued, is always just beyond our grasp, but which, if you will sit down quietly, may alight upon you.

NATHANIEL HAWTHORNE

HAPPINESS

Happy is he who by love's sweet song,
Is cheered today as he goes along.
Happier is he who believes that tomorrow
Will ease all pain and take away all sorrow,
Happiest he who on earthly sod
Has faith in himself, his friends,
    and God.

UNKNOWN

He is the happiest, be he king or peasant, who finds peace in his home.

GOETHE

The highest happiness on earth is in marriage. Every man who is happily married is a successful man even if he has failed in everything else. And every man whose marriage is a failure is not a successful man even if he has succeeded in everything else.

WILLIAM LYON PHELPS

To look fearlessly upon life; to accept the laws of nature, not with meek resignation, but as her sons, who dare to search and question; to have peace and confidence within our souls—these are the beliefs that make for happiness.

MAETERLINCK

There is a wonderful, mystical law of nature that the three things we crave most in life—happiness, freedom, and peace of mind—are always attained by giving them to someone else.

UNKNOWN

Instead of trying so hard, as some of us do, to be happy, as if that were the sole purpose of life, I would, if I were a boy again, try still harder to deserve happiness.

JAMES THOMAS FIELDS

The longer I live the more I am convinced that the one thing worth living for and dying for is the privilege of making someone more happy and more useful. No man who ever does anything to lift his fellows ever makes a sacrifice.

BOOKER T. WASHINGTON

Happiness itself is sufficient excuse. Beautiful things are right and true; so beautiful actions are those pleasing to the gods. Wise men have an inward sense of what is beautiful, and the highest wisdom is to trust this intuition and be guided by it. The answer to the last appeal of what is right lies within a man's own breast. Trust thyself.

ARISTOTLE

A long crepe veil often hides a tickled to death countenance.

R. F. OUTCAULT

There's music in the sighing of a reed;
There's music in the gushing of a rill;
There's music in all things, if men had ears
Their earth is but an echo of the spheres.

BYRON

The mate for beauty should be a man and not a money chest.

BULWER-LYTTON

If a man does not keep pace with his companions, perhaps it is because he hears a different drummer. Let him step to the music which he hears, however measured or far away.

HENRY DAVID THOREAU

All orators are dumb when beauty pleadeth.

WILLIAM SHAKESPEARE

O spirits gay, and kindly heart!
Precious the blessings ye impart!

JOANNA BAILLIE

Health

The early riser is healthy, cheerful and industrious

UNKNOWN

Joy, temperance, and repose,
Slam the door on the doctor's nose.

HENRY WADSWORTH LONGFELLOW

Be sober and temperate, and you will be healthy.

BENJAMIN FRANKLIN

Cheerfulness is health; its opposite, melancholy, is disease.

THOMAS CHANDLER HALIBURTON

I will not be as those who spend the day in complaining of the head-ache, and the night in drinking the wine that gives the head-ache.

JOHANN WOLFGANG VON GOETHE

Good humor is the health of the soul; sadness is its poison.

LESZINSKI STANISLAUS

Work is the best narcotic.

MAURICE MOLNAR

Cleanliness is a fine life-preserver.

UNKNOWN

There was never yet philosopher
That could endure the toothache patiently.

WILLIAM SHAKESPEARE

Bread is the staff of life.

JONATHAN SWIFT

If the wicked flourish, and thou suffer, be not discouraged. They are fatted for destruction: thou art dieted for health.

THOMAS FULLER

Health is, indeed, so necessary to all the duties as well as pleasures of life, that the crime of squandering it is equal to the folly; and he that for a short gratification brings weakness and diseases upon himself, and for the pleasure of a few years passed in the tumults of diversion and clamors of merriment, condemns the maturer and more experienced part of his life to the chamber and the couch, may be justly reproached, not only as a spendthrift of his happiness, but as a robber of the public; as a wretch that has voluntarily disqualified himself for the business of his station, and refused that part which Providence assigns him in the general task of human nature.

SAMUEL JOHNSON

It is not the disease but neglect of the remedy which generally destroys life.

FROM THE LATIN

They have digged their grave with their teeth.

THOMAS ADAMS

Life

He was caught in the whirl of the pool
    of dismay,
By a thoughtless remark he had said;
He had injured a friend in a nonchalant
    way,
And the love they had cherished lay dead.

To his mirror he went, in its glass to
    confide,
And his face was both haggard and pale,
And he asked of the glass, "Should I swallow
    the pride,
That is pinning me down like a nail?

Should I go to my friend with remorse on
    my face,
A remorse that I honestly feel?
Should I beg him this whirlpool of shame
    to erase,
In a soul-stirring voice of appeal?"

"As your heart so dictates," said a voice
    from the glass,
"I advise you to follow its path,
And remember 'twill pay you to keep off
    the grass,
That is bordered with ill words and wrath."

So he went to his friend, and he asked
    most sincere,
To be taken again to his heart.
And the whirlpool of friendship once
    more does endear
These friends who had drifted apart.

If there's someone you know, whom you
    treated that way,
And your heart is both heavy and blue,
Seek and find him again without further
    delay,

Don't wait until he comes to you.

*You'll find that the whirlpool of Love will
    replace*
Every misunderstanding and strife,
*It will give you the courage to meet face
    to face,*
The changeable Whirlpool of Life.

UNKNOWN

Good temper oils the wheels of life.

UNKNOWN

A sunny temper gilds the edges of life's
blackest cloud.

GUTHRIE

Melancholy is the nurse of frenzy.

WILLIAM SHAKESPEARE

O reputation! dearer far than life,
*Thou precious balsam, lovely, sweet of
    smell,*
*Whose cordial drops once spilt by some
    rash hand,*
*Not all the owner's care, not the repenting
    toil*
Of the rude spiller, ever can collect
To its first purity and native sweetness.

SIR WALTER RALEIGH

How difficult it is to save the bark of
reputation from the rocks of ignorance.

PETRARCH

How many people live on the reputation of
the reputation they might have made!

HOLMES

The die is cast.

JULIUS CAESAR

Sorrow which is never spoken is the heaviest load to bear.

BUTLER

All the world's a stage.

WILLIAM SHAKESPEARE

Plain as a nose in a man's face.

FRANCOIS RABELAIS

The greatest griefs are those we cause ourselves.

SOPHOCLES

Nothing is stronger than habit.

OVID

LIFE'S MEANING

These things make life worth while to me:
A sunset sky, a maple tree,
A mountain standing grim and gray
Against the skyline far away;
A baby's laugh, a summer breeze,
A roadway winding 'neath the trees;
A friend to trust, a book to read,
And work which meets some human need.
And through it all, a sense of God
Lifting my soul above the sod,
The hope and peace which he can give—
These make it worth my while to live.
The midnight deep in starlight still
I dreamed that I received this bill:

100

----------In account with life:
Five thousand breathless dawns all new;
Five thousand flowers fresh in dew;
Five thousand sunsets wrapped in gold;
One million snowflakes served ice cold,
Five quiet friends; one baby's love;
One white-mad sea with clouds above;
One hundred music-haunted dreams
Of moon-drenched roads and hurrying
    streams,
Of prophesying winds and trees,
Of silent stars and drowsing bees;
One June night in a fragrant wood;
One heart that loved and understood.
I wondered when I waked at day
How—how in God's name—I could pay!

COURTLAND W. SAYRES

TURN AGAIN TO LIFE

If I should die and leave you here a while,
Be not like others, sore undone, who keep
Long vigil by the silent dust and weep.
For my sake turn again to life and smile,
Nerving thy heart and trembling hand to do
That which will comfort other souls than
    thine;
Complete these dear unfinished tasks of
    mine,
And I, perchance, may therein comfort
    you.

MARY LEE HALL

LIFE

I do not like the phrase: Never cross a bridge
till you come to it. The world is owned by men
who cross bridges on their imaginations miles
and miles in advance of the procession.

BRUCE BARTON

WHAT I LIVE FOR

I live for those who love me,
  Whose Hearts are kind and true;
For the Heaven that smiles above me,
  And awaits my spirit too;
For all human ties that bind me,
  For the task by God assigned me,
For the bright hopes yet to find me,
  And the good that I can do.

I live to learn their story
  Who suffered for my sake;
To emulate their glory,
  And follow in their wake;
Bards, patriots, martyrs, sages,
The heroic of all ages,
Whose deeds crowd History's pages,
  And Time's great volume make.

I live to hold communion
  With all that is divine,
To feel there is a union
  'Twixt Nature's heart and mine;
To profit by affliction,
Reap truth from fields of fiction,
Grow wiser from conviction,
  And fulfill God's grand design.

I live to hail that season
  By gifted ones foretold,
When men shall live by reason,
  And not alone by gold;
When man to man united,
And every wrong thing righted,
The whole world shall be lighted
  As Eden was of old.

I live for those who love me,
  For those who know me true,
For the Heaven that smiles above me,
  And awaits my spirit too;
For the cause that lacks assistance,

For the wrong that needs resistance,
For the future in the distance,
   And the good that I can do.

GEORGE LINNAEUS BANKS

THE PSALM OF LIFE

Tell me not, in mournful numbers,
   Life is but an empty dream!
For the soul is dead that slumbers,
   And things are not what they seem.

Life is real! Life is earnest!
   And the grave is not its goal;
Dust thou art, to dust returnest,
   Was not spoken of the soul.

Not enjoyment, and not sorrow,
   Is our destined end or way;
But to act, that each tomorrow
   Finds us farther than today.

Art is long, and Time is fleeting,
   And our hearts, though stout and brave,
Still, like muffled drums, are beating
   Funeral marches to the grave.

In the world's broad field of battle,
   In the bivouac of life,
Be not like dumb, driven cattle!
   Be a hero in the strife!

Trust no Future, howe'er pleasant!
   Let the dead Past bury its dead!
Act—act in the living Present!
   Heart within, and God o'erhead!

Lives of great men all remind us
   We can make our lives sublime,
And, departing, leave behind us
   Footprints on the sands of time.

Footprints, that perhaps another,

Sailing o'er life's solemn main,
A forlorn and shipwrecked brother,
Seeing, shall take heart again.

Let us, then, be up and doing,
With a heart for any fate;
Still achieving, still pursuing,
Learn to labor and to wait.

HENRY WADSWORTH LONGFELLOW

Dost thou love Life? Then do not squander Time; for that's the stuff Life is made of.

BENJAMIN FRANKLIN

While there's life, there's hope.

TERENCE

LIFE'S MELODY

Life is like a keyboard. The Master's fingers will sweep over it, and a weary world will catch notes of melody as we go along. The life that is in tune with God is keyed to the note of love.

J. R. MILLER

You can't live wrong and die right.

UNKNOWN

Life is too short to be little.

DISRAELI

Life becomes tragic to him who has plenty to live on but little to live for.

UNKNOWN

KEEP YOUR OWN GATE

Have you ever watched a grower irrigate his grove, or a farmer his land? When he opens little gates to irrigation furrows there rushes in a life-giving flow of water which, in time, will result in beautiful trees and nourishing plants. Our lives are like that. Each of us is given a furrow into which flow power, wisdom, energy and health from a divine source. Like the trees and plants, we thrive—or dry up—according to the degree to which our gates are opened. But there is this tremendous difference. God lets every man be the keeper of his own gate.

UNKNOWN

To improve the golden moment of opportunity and catch the good that is within our reach, is the great art of life.

SAMUEL JOHNSON

NO STAR IS EVER LOST

Have we not all, amid life's petty strife,
Some pure ideal of a noble life
That once seemed possible? Did we not
    hear
The flutter of its wings and feel it near,
And just within our reach? It was. And yet

We lost it in this daily jar and fret.
But still our place is kept and it will wait,
Ready for us to fill it, soon or late.
No star is ever lost we once have seen:
We always may be what we might have
    been.

ADELAIDE ANNE PROCTER

The most difficult thing in life is to know yourself.

THALES

The truest end of life is to know the life that never ends.

BERESFORD

Build thee more stately mansions, O my
        soul,
As the swift seasons roll!
Leave thy low-vaulted past!
Let each new temple, nobler than the last,
Shut thee from heaven with a dome more
        vast,
Till thou at length art free,
Leaving thine outgrown shell by life's
        unresting sea!

OLIVER WENDELL HOLMES

I am not bound to win, but I am bound to be true. I am not bound to succeed, but I am bound to live by the light that I have. I must stand with anybody that stands right, stand with him while he is right, and part with him when he goes wrong.

ABRAHAM LINCOLN

The Moving Finger writes; and, having writ,
Moves on: nor all your Piety nor Wit
Shall lure it back to cancel half a Line,
Nor all your Tears wash out a Word of it.

EDWARD FITZGERALD

RECIPE FOR LIVING

Some things a man must surely know,
    If he is going to live and grow:
He needs to know that life is more

That what a man lays by in store,
That more than all he may obtain,
  Contentment offers greater gain.

He needs to feel the thrill of mirth,
  To sense the beauty of the earth,
To know the joy that kindness brings
  And all the worth of little things.
He needs to have an open mind,
  A friendly heart for all mankind,

A trust in self—without conceit—
  And strength to rise above defeat.
He needs to have the will to share,
  A mind to dream, a soul to dare,
A purpose firm, a path to plod,
  A faith in man, a trust in God.

ALFRED GRANT WALTON

GIVING AND FORGIVING

What makes life worth the living
  Is our giving and forgiving;
Giving tiny bits of kindness
  ·That will leave a joy behind us,
And forgiving bitter trifles
  That the right word often stifles,
For the little things are bigger
  Than we often stop to figure.
What makes life worth the living
  Is our giving and forgiving.

THOMAS GRANT SPRINGER

  Heaven knows we need never be ashamed of
our tears, for they are rain upon the blinding
dust of earth, overlying our hard hearts.

CHARLES DICKENS

The chain of habit coils itself around the heart like a serpent, to gnaw and stifle it.

HAZLITT

One may be humble out of pride.

MONTAIGNE

*Farewell; God knows, when we shall meet
   again,
I have a faint cold, fear thrills through my
   veins,
That almost freezes up the heat of life.*

WILLIAM SHAKESPEARE

Those that are good manners at the court are as ridiculous in the country, as the behavior of the country is most mockable at the court.

WILLIAM SHAKESPEARE

The world may be divided into people that read, people that write, people that think, and fox-hunters.

WILLIAM SHENSTONE

Architecture is the printing press of all ages, and gives a history of the state of society in which the structure was erected.

LADY SIDNEY MORGAN

Love

What's mine is yours, and what is yours is mine.

WILLIAM SHAKESPEARE

Passions, like seas, will have their ebbs and flows.

LEE

He that loveth his neighbor hath fulfilled the law.

ST. PAUL

Everyone that loveth is born of God.

ST. JOHN

There is no fear in love, but perfect love casteth out fear.

ST. JOHN

A new commandment I give unto you, That ye love one another; as I have loved you, that ye also love one another.

JOHN 13:34

Love is strong as death.

SOLOMON

This is my commandment, that ye love one another, even as I have loved you. Greater love hath no man than this: That a man lay down his life for his friends.

JESUS CHRIST

He that loveth not his brother whom he hath seen cannot love God whom he hath not seen.

ST. JOHN

Where does the family start? It starts with a young man falling in love with a girl—no superior alternative has yet been found.

SIR WINSTON CHURCHILL

I LOVE YOU

I love you not only for what you are
but for what I am when I'm with you;

I love you not only for what you have
made of yourself but what you are making
*   of me;*

I love you for putting your hand into my
heaped up heart and passing over all
the foolish weak things you can't help

dimly seeing there, and drawing out in
the light all the beautiful belongings that
no one else had looked quite far
enough to find;

I love you because you are helping me to
make of the lumber of my life not a
tavern but a temple, out of the work of
my every day life not a reproach but
a song;

I love you because you have done more
than any creed could have done to
make me good and more happy than
any fate could have done to make
me happy;

You have done it without a touch, without
a word, without a sigh;

You have done it by being yourself.

Perhaps that is what being a friend means,
after all.

UNKNOWN

When one is truly in love, one not only says
it, but shows it.

HENRY WADSWORTH LONGFELLOW

True love never grows old.

UNKNOWN

Love has no thought of self!

UNKNOWN

Love can neither be bought nor sold; its only price is love.

UNKNOWN

Let every husband stay a lover true,
And every wife remain a sweetheart too.

UNKNOWN

Good night, good night! parting is such sweet
    sorrow,
That I shall say good night till it be
    morrow.

WILLIAM SHAKESPEARE

Absence makes the heart grow fonder.

PROPERTIUS

My heart is heavy at the remembrance of all the miles that lie between us; and I can scarcely believe that you are so distant from me. We are parted; and every parting is a form of death, as every re-union is a type of heaven.

EDWARDS

Mourn not for me, for frailty is left behind. I face the next step in life's pilgrimage with the great calm with which God has so richly blessed me, knowing we are His children

112

whether we live or die, and that our deep love which endureth all things is everlasting.

ELSIE BUSH WOOLSEY

Riches take wings, comforts vanish, hope withers away, but love stays with us. God is love.

LEW WALLACE

A good husband makes a good wife.

UNKNOWN

Come, let us make love deathless, thou and I, seeing that our footing on earth is brief . . .

HERBERT FRENCH

When love and skill work together, expect a masterpiece.

CHARLES READE

Love, and a cough, cannot be hid.

GEORGE HERBERT

Grief knits two hearts in closer bonds than happiness ever can, and common suffering is a far stronger link than common joy.

ALPHONSE DE LAMARTINE

Marriages are made in heaven and consummated on earth.

JOHN LYLY

BECAUSE YOU CARE

Because you care, each task will be much
 lighter,
 Each burden so much easier to bear;
And each new morning's outlook better,
 brighter,
 And each new day more blest, because
 you care.
Because you care, each joy will seem
 completer,
 Each treasure doubly dear and true and
 rare;
And in my heart I'll always find it sweeter
 To want the higher things, because you
 care.

FRANK CRANE

Never love unless you can
Bear with all the faults of man.

THOMAS CAMPION

LOVE

Love is the sunshine of the soul. Without it
we get hard and sour and we never grow into
what we could be. Love sweetens the bitterness of experience and softens the core of
selfishness that is inherent in human nature.

UNKNOWN

Life is a flower of which love is the honey.

VICTOR HUGO

Love sacrifices all things to bless the thing it
loves.

LORD BULWER-LYTTON

Love without return is like a question without an answer.

UNKNOWN

No cord nor cable can so forcibly draw, or hold so fast, as love can do with a twined thread.

ROBERT BURTON

The first symptom of love in a young man is timidity; in a girl it is boldness. The two sexes have a tendency to approach, and each assumes the qualities of the other.

VICTOR HUGO

Love is strong as death. Many waters cannot quench love, neither can the floods drown it; if a man would give all the substance of his house for love, it would utterly be contemned.

SOLOMON

In lover's quarrels, the party that loves most is always most willing to acknowledge the greater fault.

SCOTT

Doubt thou the stars are fire!
Doubt that the sun doth move;
Doubt truth to be a liar;
But never doubt I love.

WILLIAM SHAKESPEARE

The wound's invisible
That love's keen arrows make.

WILLIAM SHAKESPEARE

Choose your love, and then love your choice.

UNKNOWN

Love makes the music of the blest above,
Heaven's harmony is universal love.

WILLIAM COWPER

Love doth ever shed rich healing where it nestles.

COBBETT

You have lived if you have loved.

ALFRED DE MUSSET

Love moderately; long love doth so;
Too swift arrives as tardy as too slow.

WILLIAM SHAKESPEARE

'Tis better to have loved and lost
Than never to have loved at all.

ALFRED, LORD TENNYSON

For oh! so wildly do I love him
That paradise itself were dim
And joyless, if not shared with him.

THOMAS MOORE

Love is a passion
Which kindles honor into noble acts.

DRYDEN

It warms me, it charms me,
   To mention but her name;
It heats me, it beats me,
   And set me a' on flame.

BURNS

Love is friendship set to music.

POLLOCK

But love is blind, and lovers cannot see
The pretty follies that themselves commit.

WILLIAM SHAKESPEARE

To write a good love-letter you ought to begin without knowing what you mean to say, and to finish without knowing what you have written.

JEAN JACQUES ROUSSEAU

What is mother's love?
A noble, pure, and tender flame
Enkindled from above.

JAMES MONTGOMERY

A mother's love!
If there be one thing pure,
Where all beside is sullied,
That can endure,
When all else passes away;
If there be aught
Surpassing human deed or word, or thought,
   It is a mother's love.

MARCHIONESS DE SPADARA

When love's well-timed, 'tis not a fault
   to love;

The strong, the brave, the virtuous, and the
*   wise,*
Sink in the soft captivity together.

ADDISON

Love is never satisfied with doing or giving anything but the best.

REV. J. M. GIBBON

Love feels no burden, thinks nothing of trouble, attempts what is above its strength, pleads no excuse of impossibility; for it thinks all things lawful for itself, and all things possible.

It is therefore able to undertake all things, and it completes many things, and brings them to a conclusion, where he who does not love, faints and lies down.

THOMAS à KEMPIS

Love is the salt of life; a higher taste
It gives to pleasure, and then makes it last.

BUCKINGHAM

All things that are on earth shall wholly
*   pass away.*
Except the love of God, which shall live
*   and last for aye.*

BRYANT

Where love is there is no labor; and if there be labor, that labor is loved.

AUSTIN

He who loves not his country can love nothing.

JOHNSON

Wherever is love and loyalty, great purposes and lofty souls, even though in a hovel or a mine, there is fairy-land.

KINGSLEY

Love did his reason blind,
And love's the noblest frailty of the mind.

DRYDEN

Love me little, love me long.

ROBERT HERRICK

It is not work that kills men; it is worry. Work is healthy; you can hardly put more upon a man than he can bear. Worry is rust upon the blade. It is not the revolution that destroys the machinery, but the friction. Fear secretes acids; but love and trust are sweet juices.

BEECHER

I am the man who, when love lectures in the heart, takes notes, and then retells the lessons to the rest of men.

DANTE ALIGHIERI

Stone walls do not a prison make,
  Nor iron bars a cage;
Minds innocent and quiet take
  That for an hermitage;
If I have freedom in my love,
  And in my soul am free,
Angels alone that soar above
  Enjoy such liberty.

RICHARD LOVELACE

LOVE

Because you love me all my life
  Is circled with unquestioned rest;

Yes, even Life and even Death
  Is all unquestioned and all blest.

I hold it true what 'er befall;
  I feel it when I sorrow most;
  'Tis better to have loved and lost
Than never to have loved at all.

ALFRED, LORD TENNYSON

HOW DO I LOVE THEE

How do I love thee? Let me count the ways.
I love thee to the depth and breadth and
      height
My soul can reach, when feeling out of
      sight
For the ends of Being and ideal Grace.
I love thee to the level of everyday's
Most quiet need, by sun and candle-light.
I love thee freely, as men strive for Right;
I love thee purely, as they turn from Praise.
I love thee with the passion put to use
In my old griefs, and with my childhood's
      faith.
I love thee with a love I seemed to lose
With my lost saints—I love thee with the
      breath,
Smiles, tears, of all my life!—and, if God
      choose,
I shall but love thee better after death.

ELIZABETH BARRETT BROWNING

To love is the great Amulet that makes this
world a garden.

ROBERT LOUIS STEVENSON

Oh! how many torments lie in the small
circle of a wedding ring.

COLLEY CIBBER

WHAT IS LOVE?

It's silence when your words would hurt,
It's patience when your neighbor's curt.
It's deafness when the scandal flows,
It's thoughtfulness for another's woes.
It's promptness when stern duty calls,
It's courage when misfortune falls.

UNKNOWN

MAKE IT UP

Life is too short for grievances—
For quarrels and for tears,
What's the use of wasting
Precious days and precious tears.

If there's something to forgive—
Forgive without delay—
Maybe you, too, were part to blame,
So make it up today.

Be generous—forget the past
And take the broader view,
Cast away all bitterness and
Let the sunshine through.

If it's within your power
A broken heart to mend,
Remember—Love is all that
Really matters—in the end.

UNKNOWN

THOSE WE LOVE THE BEST

They say the world is round, and yet
  I often think it square,

So many little hurts we get
  From corners here and there.
But one great truth in life I've found,
  While journeying to the West—
The only folks we really wound
  Are those we love the best.

The man you thoroughly despise
  Can rouse your wrath, 'tis true;
Annoyance in your heart will rise
  At things mere strangers do;
But those are only passing ills;
  This rule all lives will prove;
The rankling wound which aches and
    thrills
  Is dealt by hands we love.

The choicest garb, the sweetest grace,
  Are oft to strangers shown;
The careless mien, the frowning face,
  Are given to our own.
We flatter those we scarcely know,
  We please the fleeting guest,
And deal full many a thoughtless blow
  To those who love us best.

Love does not grow on every tree,
  Nor true hearts yearly bloom.
Alas for those who only see
  This cut across a tomb!
But, soon or late, the fact grows plain
  To all through sorrow's test:
The only folks who give us pain
  Are those we love the best.

ELLA WHEELER WILCOX

Love is not one of the attributes of God, but
the sum of them all.

REV. J. M. GIBBON

Love is a hammer that will break the hardest
heart.

UNKNOWN

TELL HER SO

Amid the cares of married strife,
In spite of toil and business life,
If you value your sweet wife,
   Tell her so!

When days are dark and deeply blue,
She has her troubles, same as you.
Show her that your love is true—
   Tell her so!

There was a time you thought it bliss
To get the favor of one kiss;
A dozen now won't come amiss—
   Tell her so!

Don't act, if she has passed her prime,
As tho' to please her were a crime;
If ever you loved her, now's the time—
   Tell her so!

She'll return, for each caress,
An hundredfold of tenderness!
Hearts like hers were made to bless!
   Tell her so.

You are hers and hers alone;
Well you know she's all your own;
Don't wait to carve it on a stone—
   Tell her so.

Never let her heart grow cold—
Richer beauties will unfold;
She is worth her weight in gold!
   Tell her so.

UNKNOWN

A house is built of logs and stone,
   Of tiles and posts and piers;
A home is built of loving deeds
   That stand a thousand years.

VICTOR HUGO

Grief can take care of itself, but to get the full value of a joy you must have somebody to divide it with.

MARK TWAIN

Entreat me not to leave thee,
   Or to return from following after thee:
For whither thou goest, I will go;
   And where thou lodgest, I will lodge:
Thy people shall be my people,
   And thy God my God;
Where thou diest, will I die,
   And there will I be buried;
The Lord do so to me,
And more also,
   If naught but death part thee and me.

RUTH 1:16-17

Love's like the measles—all the worse when it comes late in life.

JERROLA

Man

When a man finds not repose in himself it is in vain for him to seek it elsewhere.

FROM THE FRENCH

The true test of a civilization is not the census, nor the size of cities, nor the crops—no, but the kind of man the country turns out.

BENJAMIN DISRAELI

May the outward and the inner man be as one.

SOCRATES

I see that fashion wears out more apparel than the man.

WILLIAM SHAKESPEARE

MY CREED

To live as gently as I can;
To be, no matter where, a man;
To take what comes of good or ill
And cling to faith and honor still;
To do my best, and let that stand;
The record of my brain and hand;
And then, should failure come to me,
Still work and hope for victory.

To have no secret place wherein
I stoop unseen to shame or sin;
To be the same when I'm alone
As when my every deed is known;
To live undaunted, unafraid
Of any step that I have made;
To be without pretense or sham
Exactly what men think I am.

To leave some simple mark behind
To keep my having lived in mind;
If enmity to aught I show,
To be an honest, generous foe,
To play my little part, nor whine

That greater honors are not mine.
This, I believe is all I need
For my philosophy and creed.

EDGAR A. GUEST

Man's rich with little, were his judgment true;
Nature is frugal, and her wants are few;
These few wants, answer'd bring sincere
    delights;
But fools create themselves new appetites.

YOUNG

   Speech is a mirror of the soul: as a man
speaks, so is he.

PUBLIUS SYRUS

Friends, Romans, countrymen, lend me your
    ears;
I come to bury Caesar, not to praise him.
The evil that men do lives after them,
The good is oft interred with their bones.

WILLIAM SHAKESPEARE

   The greatest truths are the simplest: so are
the greatest men.

UNKNOWN

Every man is the architect of his own fortune.

APPIUS CLAUDIUS CAECUS

Appearances deceive. And this one maxim is a standing rule: Men are not what they seem.

HARVARD

He that complies against his will
Is of the same opinion still.

SAMUEL BUTLER

A light supper, a good night's sleep and a fine morning have often made a hero of the same man, who, by indigestion, a restless night and a rainy morning would have proved a coward.

EARL OF CHESTERFIELD

It is better for a city to be governed by a good man than by good laws.

ARISTOTLE

A man should not allow himself to hate even his enemies, because if you indulge this passion, on some occasions, it will rise of itself in others: if you hate your enemies, you will contract such a vicious habit of mind, as by degrees will break out upon those who are your friends, or those who are indifferent to you.

PLUTARCH

In my stars I am above thee, but be not afraid of greatness: some are born great, some achieve greatness, and some have greatness thrust upon them.

WILLIAM SHAKESPEARE

A man must first govern himself ere he be fit to govern a family, and his family ere he be fit to bear the government of the commonwealth.

SIR WALTER RALEIGH

Hope springs eternal in the human breast:
Man never is, but always to be blest.

ALEXANDER POPE

A man he seems of cheerful yesterdays and confident tomorrows.

WILLIAM WORDSWORTH

Know then thyself, presume not God to
    scan;
The proper study of mankind is man.

ALEXANDER POPE

Never have anything to do with an unlucky place, or an unlucky man. I have seen many clever men, very clever men, who had not shoes to their feet. I never act with them. Their advice sounds very well, but they cannot get on themselves; and if they cannot do good to themselves, how can they do good to me?

MAYER A. ROTHSCHILD

It is far easier to know men than to know man.

DUC DE LA ROCHEFOUCAULD

Men are the sport of circumstances, when the circumstances seem the sport of men.

LORD BYRON

Since the generality of persons act from impulse much more than from principle, men are neither so good nor so bad as we are apt to think them.

AUGUST W. HARE

Never has a man who has bent himself been able to make others straight.

MENCIUS

Man is a prisoner who has no right to open the door of his prison and run away ... A man should wait, and not take his own life until God summons him.

PLATO

Men trust their ears less than their eyes.

HERODOTUS

Nobody likes the man who brings bad news.

SOPHOCLES

An obstinate man does not hold opinions, but they hold him.

ALEXANDER POPE

He that never changed any of his opinions never corrected any of his mistakes; and he who was never wise enough to find out any mistakes in himself will not be charitable enough to excuse what he reckons mistakes in others.

UNKNOWN

IF

If you can keep your head when all about you

Are losing theirs and blaming it on you;
If you can trust yourself when all men
    doubt you,
  But make allowances for their doubting
    too;
If you can wait and not be tired by waiting
  Or, being lied about, don't deal in lies,
Or, being hated, don't give way to hating,
  And yet don't look too good, nor talk
    too wise;
If you can dream—and not make dreams
    your master;
  If you can think—and not make thoughts
    your aim;
If you can meet with triumph and disaster
  And treat those two imposters just the
    same;
If you can bear to hear the truth you've
    spoken
  Twisted by knaves to make a trap for
    fools,
Or watch the things you gave your life to
    broken,
  And stoop and build 'em up with
    worn-out tools;
If you can make one heap of all your
    winnings
  And risk it on one turn of pitch-and-
    toss,
And lose, and start again at your beginnings
  And never breathe a word about your
    loss;
If you can force your heart and nerve
    and sinew
  To serve your turn long after they are
    gone,
And so hold on when there is nothing
    in you
  Except the will which says to them:
  "Hold on";
If you can talk with crowds and keep
    your virtue,
  Or walk with kings—nor lose the commons

touch;

If neither foes nor loving friends can hurt
  you;
  If men count with you, but none too
  much;
If you can fill the unforgiving minute
  With sixty seconds worth of distance
  run—
Yours is the earth and everything that's
  in it,
  And—which is more—you'll be a Man,
  my son!

RUDYARD KIPLING

He is the whole encyclopedia of facts. The
creation of a thousand forests is in one acorn;
and Egypt, Greece, Rome, Gaul, Britain,
America, lie folded already in the first man.

EMERSON

Some men put me in mind of half-bred
horses, which often grow worse in proportion
as you feed and exercise them for improvement.

GREVILLE

To arrive at perfection, a man should have
very sincere friends or inveterate enemies;
because he would be made sensible of his good
or ill conduct, either by the censures of the one,
or the admonitions of the other.

DIOGENES

To many men well-fitting doors are not set
on their tongues.

THEOGENIS

To feel for none is the true social art
Of the world's stoics—men without a
    heart.

LORD BYRON

Man never fastened one end of a chain
around the neck of his brother, that God's own
hand did not fasten the other end round the
neck of the oppressor.

LAMARTINE

No man was ever so much deceived by
another as by himself.

GREVILLE

The best laid schemes o' mice and men,
    Gang aft a-gley,
And lea'e us nought but grief and pain,
    For promised joy.

ROBERT BURNS

Of all mankind, each loves himself the best.

TERENCE

Speak but little and well, if you would be
esteemed as a man of merit.

TRENCH

A bad husband cannot be a good man.

UNKNOWN

It is quite absurd to say that a man is good or
bad—he is good and bad.

ELBERT HUBBARD

Every man has his little weakness. It often takes the form of a desire to get something for nothing.

ELBERT HUBBARD

The great man is he who does not lose his child's-heart.

MENCIUS

I am a man: nothing human is alien to me.

TERENCE

For want of a nail the shoe is lost, for want of a shoe the horse is lost, for want of a horse the rider is lost.

GÉORGE HERBERT

No man can safely go abroad who does not love to stay at home.

THOMAS à KEMPIS

He experienced that nervous agitation to which brave men as well as cowards are subject; with this difference, that the one sinks under it, like the vine under the hailstorm, and the other collects his energies to shake it off, as the cedar of Lebanon is said to elevate its boughs to disperse the snow which accumulates upon them.

SIR WALTER SCOTT

The superior man is satisfied and composed; the mean man is always full of distress.

CONFUCIUS

Nobody knows what a boy is worth, and the world must wait and see; for every man in an honored place, is a boy that used to be.

UNKNOWN

As a man thinketh in his heart, so is he.

BIBLE (PROVERBS)

Whosoever commands the sea commands the trade; whosoever commands the trade of the world commands the riches of the world, and, consequently, the world itself.

SIR WALTER RALEIGH

He whose pride oppresses the humble may, perhaps, be humbled, but will never be humble.

LAVATER

Blessed is the man that walketh not in the counsel of the ungodly, nor standeth in the way of sinners, nor sitteth in the seat of the scornful.

DAVID

An oath is not needed by a good man, nor will it prevent the bad man from perjuring himself.

W. H. HOWE

Victory shifts from man to man.

HOMER

The balls of sight are so formed, that one man's eyes are spectacles to another, to read his heart within.

SAMUEL JOHNSON

The depth of one's convictions measures the breadth of his influence.

UNKNOWN

CHARACTER

Character is like a tree and reputation is like its shadow. The shadow is what we think of it; the tree is the real thing.

ABRAHAM LINCOLN

It is not what he has, nor even what he does, which directly affects the worth of a man; but what he is.

HENRI-FREDERIC AMIEL

Great men never feel great; small men never feel small.

UNKNOWN

Manners maketh man.

WILLIAM OF WYKEHAM

Nothing, indeed, but the possession of some power can with any certainty discover what at the bottom is the true character of any man.

BURKE

LOVE OF COUNTRY

Breathes there the man, with soul so dead,
Who never to himself hath said,
This is my own, my native land!
Whose heart hath ne'er within him burn'd,
As home his footsteps he hath turn'd
From wandering on a foreign strand!
If such there breathe, go, mark him well;
For him no Minstrel raptures swell;
High though his titles, proud his name,
Boundless his wealth as wish can claim;
Despite those titles, power, and pelf,
The wretch, concentered all in self,
Living, shall forfeit fair renown,
And, doubly dying, shall go down
To the vile dust, from whence he sprung,
Unwept, unhonor'd, and unsung.

SIR WALTER SCOTT

The reputation of a man is like his shadow: gigantic when it precedes him, and pigmy in its proportions when it follows.

CHARLES MAURICE DE TALLEYRAND-PERIGORD

Man proposes, but God disposes.

THOMAS à KEMPIS

Every man has in himself a continent of undiscovered character. Happy he who acts the Columbus to his own soul!

STEPHEN

THE DOOMED MAN

There is a time, we know not when,
A point we know not where,

That marks the destiny of men,
   For glory or despair.

There is a line, by us unseen,
   That crosses every path;
The hidden boundary between
   God's patience and His wrath.

JOSEPH ADDISON ALEXANDER

God taught mankind on that first Christmas
   day
What 'twas to be a man; to give, not take;
To serve, not rule; to nourish, not devour;
To help, not crush; if need, to die, not live.

CHARLES KINGSLEY

Every man for himself and God for us all.

JOHN HEYWOOD

THE GUY IN THE GLASS

If you get what you want in struggle for self;
   And the world makes you king for a day;
Then go to the mirror and look at yourself,
   And see what the guy has to say.

For it isn't your father, your mother, or wife,
   Who judgment on you must pass;
The fellow whose verdict counts most in
    your life
   Is the guy staring back from the glass.

He's the fellow to please, never mind all
   the rest,
   For he's with you clear to the end;

You have passed your dangerous difficult
 task,
 If the guy in the glass is your friend.

You must be like Jack Horner and chisel
 a plum,
 And you think you're a wonderful guy;
But the man in the glass says: "You're a
 bum,"
 If you can't look him straight in the eye.

You may fool the whole world down the
 pathway of years
 And get pats on your back as you pass;
But your final reward will be heartaches
 and tears,
 If you've cheated the guy in the glass.

OSCAR R. GRUTER

Beware the fury of a patient man.

JOHN DRYDEN

Men are but children of a larger growth.

DRYDEN

Men are born with two eyes, but with one
tongue, in order that they should see twice as
much as they say.

CHARLES CALEB COLTON

Every man is a volume, if you know how to
read him.

WILLIAM ELLERY CHANNING

'Tis easy enough to be pleasant,
When life flows by like a song;
But the man worth while,
Is the man with a smile,
When everything goes dead wrong.

ELLA WHEELER WILCOX

Man is a bundle of habits.

PALEY

The man who has not anything to boast of but his illustrious ancestors, is like a potato—the only thing belonging to him is under ground.

SIR THOMAS OVERBURY

He that would govern others, first should be Master of himself.

PHILIP MASSINGER

We may live without poetry, music and
        art;
We may live without conscience, and live
        without heart;
We may live without friends; we may
        live without books;
But civilized man cannot live without
        cooks.
He may live without books—what is
        knowledge but grieving?
He may live without hope—what is hope
        but deceiving?
He may live without love—what is passion
        but pining?
But where is the man that can live
        without dining?

EDWARD ROBERT BULWER-LYTTON

Never shrink from doing anything which your business calls you to do. The man who is above his business, may one day find his business above him.

SAMUEL DREW

Man is born to act. To act is to affirm the worth of an end, and to affirm the worth of an end, is to create an ideal.

OLIVER WENDELL HOLMES

Words show the wit of man, but actions his meaning.

UNKNOWN

Lord, what fools these mortals be!

WILLIAM SHAKESPEARE

AM I A BUILDER?

I watched them tearing a building down,
  A gang of men in a busy town.
With a ho-heave-ho and a lusty yell
  They swung a beam, and the side wall fell.
I asked the foreman, "Are these men skilled,
  And the men you'd hire if you had to
    build?"

He gave a laugh and said: "No indeed!
  Just common labor is all I need.
I can easily wreck in a day or two
  What builders have taken a year to do."
And I thought to myself as I went away,
  Which of these roles have I tried to play?

140

Am I a builder who works with care,
  Measuring life by the rule and square?
Am I shaping my deeds to a well-made plan,
  Patiently doing the best I can?
Or am I a wrecker, who walks the town
  Content with the labor of tearing down?

UNKNOWN

MYSELF

I have to live with myself, and so
I want to be fit for myself to know,
I want to be able, as days go by,
Always to look myself straight in the eye;
I don't want to stand, with the setting sun,
And hate myself for the things I have done.

I don't want to keep on a closet shelf
A lot of secrets about myself,
And fool myself, as I come and go,
Into thinking that nobody else will know
The kind of a man I really am;
I don't want to dress up myself in sham.

I want to go out with my head erect,
I want to deserve all men's respect;
But here in the struggle for fame and pelf
I want to be able to like myself.
I don't want to look at myself and know
That I'm bluster and bluff and empty show.

I can never hide myself from me;
I see what others may never see;
I know what others may never know,
I never can fool myself, and so,
Whatever happens, I want to be
Self-respecting and conscience free.

EDGAR A. GUEST

A man is a great thing upon the earth and through eternity, but every jot of the greatness of man is unfolded out of woman.

WALT WHITMAN

If thou art a master, be sometimes blind; if a servant, be sometimes deaf.

THOMAS FULLER

Fellows who have no tongues are often all eyes and ears.

HALIBURTON

The best merchants never best each other.

UNKNOWN

A politician, Proteus-like must alter
His face, and habit; and, like water, seem
Of the same color that the vessel is
That doth contain it; varying his form
With the chameleon at each object's change.

MASON

Woodman, spare that tree!
  Touch not a single bough!
In youth it sheltered me,
  And I'll protect it now.

GEORGE POPE MORRIS

Defeated, but not dismayed—crushed to the earth, but not humiliated,—he seemed to grow more haughty beneath disaster, and to experience a fierce satisfaction in draining the last dregs of bitterness.

WASHINGTON IRVING

His face was of the doubtful kind;
That wins the eye and not the mind.

SCOTT

And oftener changed their principles than their shirts.

DR. YOUNG

A fool, indeed, has great need of a title,
It teaches men to call him count and duke,
And to forget his proper name of fool.

JOHN CROWNE

I am but a gatherer and disposer of other men's stuff.

SIR HENRY WOTTON

There are but three classes of men: *the retrograde, the stationary* and *the progressive.*

LAVATER

The Mind

TWENTY YEARS AGO

I've wandered to the village, Tom, I've sat
    beneath the tree,
Upon the schoolhouse playground, which
    sheltered you and me,
But none were there to greet me, Tom, and
    few were left to know,
That played with us upon the grass some
    twenty years ago.

The grass is just as green, Tom—barefooted
    boys at play
Were sporting just as we did then, with
    spirits just as gay;
But the "master" sleeps upon the hill,
    which, coated o'er with snow
Afforded us a sliding place, just twenty
    years ago.

The old schoolhouse is alter'd some, the
    benches are replaced
By new ones, very like the same our
    penknives had defaced,
But the same old bricks are in the wall,
    the bell swings to and fro,
It's music, just the same, dear Tom, 'twas
    twenty years ago.

The boys were playing the same old
    game, beneath the same old tree—
I do forget the name just now; you've
    played the same with me
On that same spot; 'twas played with
    knives, by throwing so and so,
The loser had a task to do, just twenty
    years ago.

The river's running just as still, the willows
    on its side
Are larger than they were, Tom, the stream
    appears less wide.
But the grape-vine swing is ruin'd now
    where once we played the beau,
And swung our sweethearts—"pretty girls"
    —just twenty years ago.

The spring that bubbled 'neath the hill,
    close by the spreading beech,
Is very low—'twas once so high that we
    could almost reach;
And kneeling down to get a drink,
    dear Tom, I even started so!
To see how much that I am changed
    since twenty years ago.

Nearby the spring, upon an elm, you know
    I cut your name,
Your sweetheart's just beneath it, Tom,
    and you did mine the same—
Some heartless wretch had peel'd the bark,
    'twas dying sure but slow,
Just as the one whose name was cut, died
    twenty years ago.

My lids have long been dry, Tom, but
    tears came in my eyes,
I thought of her I loved so well—those
    early broken ties—
I visited the old churchyard, and took
    some flowers to strew
Upon the graves of those we loved,
    some twenty years ago.

Some are in the churchyard laid, some
　　sleep beneath the sea
But few are left of our old class, excepting
　　you and me,
And when our time is come, Tom, and
　　we are called to go.
I hope they'll lay us where we played,
　　just twenty years ago.

A. J. GAULT

THINK

If you think you are beaten, you are;
　　If you think you dare not, you don't;
If you'd like to win, but think you can't,
　　It's almost a cinch you won't.

If you think you'll lose, you're lost,
　　For out in the world we find
Success begins with a fellow's WILL—
　　It's all in the state of mind.

If you think you're outclassed, you are;
　　You've got to think high to rise.
You've just got-to-be sure of yourself
　　Before you can win the prize.

Life's battles don't always go
　　To the stronger or faster man,
But sooner or later the man who wins
　　Is the one who THINKS HE CAN.

UNKNOWN

Stone walls do not a prison make,
　　Nor iron bars a cage;
Minds innocent and quiet take
　　That for an hermitage.

RICHARD LOVELACE

They always talk who never think.

MATTHEW PRIOR

Order is the sanity of the mind, the health of the body, the peace of the city, the security of the state. As the beams to a house, as the bones to the microcosm of man, so is order to all things.

ROBERT SOUTHEY

PATRIOTISM

A thoughtful mind . . .
  sees not the flag only,
but the nation itself . . .
  the principles, the truths,
  the history.

HENRY WARD BEECHER

THINK

Harsh words, like chickens, love to stray
But they come home to rest each day . . .
If you have angry words to say . . .
  Stop and think!
The world will judge you by your deeds;
They can be flowers, fair, or weeds . . .
Before you plant those tiny seeds . . .
  Stop and think!
God gave us each a heart for song;
A brain to reason right from wrong . . .
So, when temptation gets too strong . . .
  Stop and think!

UNKNOWN

Quiet minds can not be perplexed or frightened, but go on in fortune or misfortune at their own private pace, like a clock during a thunderstorm.

ROBERT LOUIS STEVENSON

The thought,
The deadly thought of solitude.

KEATS

It is one thing to purloin finely-tempered steel, and another to take a pound of literary old iron, and convert it in the furnace of one's mind into a hundred watchsprings, worth each a thousand times as much as the iron. When genius borrows, it borrows grandly, giving to the borrowed matter, a life and beauty it lacked before.

ANON.

If he had two ideas in his head, they would fall out with each other.

JOHNSON

Wit and judgment often are at strife,
Though meant to be each other's aid like
*   man and wife.*

POPE

Words are things; and a small drop of ink,
Falling like dew upon a thought, produces
That which makes thousands, perhaps
*   millions, think.*

BYRON

Restrain thy mind, and let mildness ever

attend thy tongue.

THEOGENIS

Any mind that is capable of a *real sorrow* is capable of good.

MRS. STOWE

I think, therefore I am.

RÉNE DESCARTES

Thoughts are but dreams till their effects be tried.

WILLIAM SHAKESPEARE

There's nothing good or bad, but thinking makes it so.

WILLIAM SHAKESPEARE

There are very few original thinkers in the world; the greatest part of those who are called philosophers have adopted the opinions of some who went before them.

DUGALD STEWART

Apt words have power to suage
The tumors of a troubled mind
And are as balm to fester'd wounds.

JOHN MILTON

Man is a thinking being, whether he will or no: all he can do is to turn his thoughts the best way.

SIR WILLIAM TEMPLE

It is not enough to have a good mind. The main thing is to use it well.

RENE DESCARTES

The temple of our purest thoughts is—silence!

SARAH JOSEPHA HALE

In this world second thoughts, it seems, are best.

EURIPIDES

Ye tradeful merchants that with weary toil,
Do seek most precious things to make you
    gaine,
And both the Indies of their treasures
    spoil;
What needeth you to seek so far in vain?
For lo! my love doth in herself contain
All this world's riches that may far be
    found;
If saphyrs, lo! her eyes be saphyrs plain;
If rubies, lo her lips be rubies sound;
If pearls, her teeth be pearls, both pure
    and round;
If ivory, her forehead's ivory I ween;
If gold, her locks are finest gold on ground;
If silver, her fair hands are silver sheen;
But that which fairest is, but few behold,
Her mind, adorn'd with virtues manifold.

SPENSER

Ah! noblest minds
Sink soonest into ruin; like a tree,
That with the weight of its own golden fruitage
Is bent down to the dust.

HENRY NEELE

I know nothing except the fact of my ignorance.

SOCRATES

Narrowness of mind is often the cause of obstinacy: we do not easily believe beyond what we see.

DUC DE LA ROCHEFOUCAULD

As the language of the face is universal, so 'tis very comprehensive; no laconism can reach it: 'tis the short hand of the mind, and crowds a great deal in a little room.

JEREMY COLLIER

Reason is God's crowning gift to man.

SOPHOCLES

My mind to me an empire is.

SOUTHWELL

Cultivation to the mind is as necessary as food to the body.

CICERO

A mind content both crown and kingdom is.

ROBERT GREENE

It is the mind that maketh good or ill,
That maketh wretch or happy, rich or
poor.

EDMUND SPENSER

I hardly know so true a mark of a little mind as the servile imitation of another.

GREVILLE

The mind ought sometimes to be diverted, that it may return the better to thinking.

PHAEDRUS

A weak mind is like a microscope, which magnifies trifling things, but cannot receive great ones.

EARL OF CHESTERFIELD

He listens well who takes notes.

DANTE ALIGHIERI

'Tis the mind that makes the body rich.

WILLIAM SHAKESPEARE

To the memory of the Man, first in war, first in peace, and first in the hearts of his countrymen.

HENRY LEE

He who has not a good memory, should never take upon him the trade of lying.

MONTAIGNE

A man thinks with his memory.

UNKNOWN

UNCONSCIOUS CEREBRATION

Say not that the past is dead.
Though the Autumn leaves are shed,
Though the day's last flush has flown,
Though the lute has lost its tone—
Still within, unfelt, unseen.
Lives the life that once has been;
With a silent power still
Guiding heart or brain or will.
Lending bias, force and hue
To the things we think and do.
Strange! how aimless looks or words
Sometimes wake forgotten chords,
Bidding dreams and memories leap
From a long unbroken sleep.

WILLIAM EDWARD HARTPOLE LECKY

MEMORY

When time, which steals our years away,
Shall·steal our pleasures too;
The memory of the past will stay
And half our joys renew.

UNKNOWN

MEMORY

Music, when soft voices die,
Vibrates in the memroy;
Odors, when sweet violets sicken,
Live within the sense they quicken.

Rose leaves, when the rose is dead,
Are heaped for the beloved's bed;
And so thy thoughts, when thou art gone,
Love itself shall slumber on.

PERCY BYSSHE SHELLEY

REMEMBER

Remember me when I am gone away,
  Gone far away into the silent land;
  When you can no more hold me by the
    hand,
Nor I half turn to go, yet turning stay.
Remember me when no more, day by day,
  You tell me of our future that you
    planned:
  Only remember me; you understand
It will be late to counsel then or pray.
Yet if you should forget me for a while
  And afterwards remember, do not grieve:
  For if the darkness and corruption leave
  A vestige of the thoughts that once I had,
Better by far you should forget and smile
  Than that you should remember and be
    sad.

CHRISTINA GEORGINA ROSETTI

MEMORY

Into my heart's treasury
  I slipped a coin,
That time cannot rust
  Nor a thief purloin;
Oh better than the minting
  Of a gold-crowned king
Is the safe-kept memory
  Of a lovely thing.

SARA TEASDALE

Look not mournfully into the Past. It comes
not back again. Wisely improve the Present. It

is thine. Go forth to meet the shadowy Future, without fear, and with a manly heart.

HENRY WADSWORTH LONGFELLOW

OFT, IN THE STILLY NIGHT

Oft in the stilly night,
Ere Slumber's chain has bound me,
Fond Memory brings the light
Of other days around me,
The smiles, the tears
Of boyhood's years,
The words of love then spoken;
The eyes that shone,
Now dimmed and gone,
The cheerful hearts now broken!
Thus, in the stilly night,
Ere Slumber's chain has bound me,
Sad Memory brings the light
Of other days around me.

When I remember all
The friends, so linked together,
I've seen around me fall,
Like leaves in wintry weather;
I feel like one
Who treads alone
Some banquet hall deserted,
Whose lights are fled,
Whose garlands dead,
And all but he departed.
Thus, in the stilly night,
Ere Slumber's chain has bound me,
Sad Memory brings the light
Of other days around me.

THOMAS MOORE

Every one complains of the badness of his memory, but nobody of his judgment.

DUC DE LA ROCHEFOUCAULD

It isn't the things that go in one ear and out the other that hurt, as much as the things that go in one ear and get all mixed up before they slip out the mouth.

UNKNOWN

One ear heard it, and at the other out it went.

GEOFFREY CHAUCER

Think all you speak, but speak not all you think.

UNKNOWN

Ignorance is the night of the mind, but a night without moon or star.

CONFUCIUS

But, for my own part, it was Greek to me.

WILLIAM SHAKESPEARE

FROM "THANATOPSIS"

So live that when thy summons comes to
*   join*
The innumerable caravan which moves
To that mysterious realm where each shall
*   take*
His chamber in the silent halls of death,
Thou go not, like the quarry-slave at night,
Scourged to his dungeon, but, sustained
*   and soothed*
By an unfaltering trust, approach thy grave
Like one who wraps the drapery of his
*   couch*

About him, and lies down to pleasant
   dreams.

WILLIAM CULLEN BRYANT

Appearances are often deceiving.

AESOP

Horses will do more for a whistle than for a whip.

THOMAS FULLER

The best colt needs breaking in.

UNKNOWN

His bark is worse than his bite.

GEORGE HERBERT

We are not sent into this world to do anything into which we can not put our hearts. We have certain work to do for our bread and that is to be done strenuously, other work to do for our delight and that is to be done heartily; neither is to be done by halves or shifts, but with a will, and what is not worth this effort is not to be done at all.

JOHN RUSKIN

Thy wish was father, Harry, to that thought.

WILLIAM SHAKESPEARE

Money

Rich, not be exalted; poor, be not dejected.

CLEOBULUS

As riches and favor forsake a man, we discover him to be a fool, but nobody could find it out in his prosperity.

LA BRUYÈRE

Every man was not born with a silver spoon in his mouth.

MIGUEL DE CERVANTES

Beware of little expenses; a small leak will sink a great ship.

BENJAMIN FRANKLIN

The only way for a rich man to be healthy is, by exercise and abstinence, to live as if he were poor.

SIR WILLIAM TEMPLE

He who marries for wealth sells his own liberty.

UNKNOWN

The difference between a rich man and a poor man is this—the former eats when he pleases, and the latter when he can get it.

SIR WALTER RALEIGH

When articles rise, the consumer is the first that suffers, and when they fall, he is the last that gains.

COLTON

It is far more easy to acquire a fortune like a knave than to expend it like a gentleman.

COLTON

If you make money your god, it will plague you like the devil.

HENRY FIELDING

A fool and his money are soon parted.

UNKNOWN

There is nothing that makes men rich and strong but that which they carry inside of them. Wealth is of the heart, not of the hand.

JOHN MILTON

*For what is worth in anything
But so much money as 'twill bring?*

SAMUEL BUTLER

A penny for your thought.

JOHN HEYWOOD

He hath riches sufficient, who hath enough to be charitable.

SIR THOMAS BROWNE

A money-lender. He serves you in the present tense; he lends you in the conditional mood;

keeps you in the subjunctive; and ruins you in the future!

ADDISON

It's not what you'd do with a million,
If riches should e'er be your lot,
But what are you doing at present
With the dollar and a half you've got?

UNKNOWN

Paid him in his own coin.

MIGUEL DE CERVANTES

Everything is worth what its purchaser will pay for it.

PUBLIUS SYRUS

He is poor whose expenses exceed his income.

LA BRUYÈRE

Live within your means.

UNKNOWN

The greatest wealth is contentment with a little.

UNKNOWN

Economy is of itself a great revenue.

CICERO

Better go to bed supperless than rise in debt.

Money is a good servant, but a dangerous master.

BONHOURS

He that wants money, means and content, is without three good friends.

WILLIAM SHAKESPEARE

Put not your trust in money, but put your money in trust.

OLIVER WENDELL HOLMES

A great fortune is a great slavery.

SENECA

For they say, if money go before, all ways do lie open.

WILLIAM SHAKESPEARE

For the love of money is the root of all evil; which while some coveted after, they have erred from the faith, and pierced themselves through with many sorrows.

I TIM. VI, 10

A penny saved is a penny earned.

UNKNOWN

That which we acquire with the most difficulty we retain the longest; as those who have earned a fortune are usually more careful of it than those who have inherited one.

COLTON

He that does not save pennies will never have dollars.

UNKNOWN

Thy credit wary keep, 'tis quickly gone:
Being got by many actions, lost by one.

RANDOLPH

The way to wealth is as plain as the way to market. It depends chiefly on two words, industry and frugality; that is, waste neither time nor money, but make the best use of both. Without industry and frugality, nothing will do; and with them, everything.

BENJAMIN FRANKLIN

Things sweet to taste, prove in digestion sour.

WILLIAM SHAKESPEARE

Rome was not built in one day.

JOHN HEYWOOD

A felon's cell—
The fittest earthy type of hell!

JOHN GREENLEAF WHITTIER

Music

Where words fail, music speaks.

HANS CHRISTIAN ANDERSON

Melody has by Beethoven been freed from the influence of Fashion and changing Taste, and raised to an ever-valid, purely human type. Beethoven's music will be understood to all time, while that of his predecessors will, for the most part, only remain intelligible to us through the medium of reflection on the history of art.

RICHARD WAGNER

Music was a thing of the soul—a rose-lipped shell that murmured of the eternal sea—a strange bird singing the songs of another shore.

J. C. HOLLAND

What is music? This question occupied my mind for hours last night before I fell asleep. The very existence of music is wonderful, I might even say miraculous. Its domain is between thought and phenomena. Like a twilight mediator, it hovers between spirit and matter, related to both, yet differing from each. It is spirit, but spirit subject to the measurement of time: It is matter, but matter that can dispense with space.

HEINRICH HEINE

Music is well said to be the speech of angels.

THOMAS CARLYLE

FOLK MUSIC

They chant their artless notes in simple guise. They tune their hearts, by far the noblest aim.

ROBERT BURNS

Life has loveliness to sell,
  Music like a curve of gold,
Scent of pine trees in the rain,
  Eyes that love you, arms that hold,
And for your spirit's still delight,
  Holy thoughts that star the night.

SARA TEASDALE

The most difficult of all musical instruments to learn to play is the second fiddle.

UNKNOWN

Would you have your songs endure?
Build on the human heart.

ROBERT BROWNING

Music hath charms to soothe a savage breast,
To soften rocks, or bend a knotted oak.
I've read that things inanimate have moved,
And as with living souls have been inform'd
By magic numbers and persuasive sound.

WILLIAM CONGREVE

The meaning of a song goes deep. Who is there that, in logical words, can express the effect music has on us?

THOMAS CARLYLE

MUSIC

How many of us stop to think
Of music as a wondrous magic link
With God; taking sometimes the place of
    prayer,
When words have failed us 'neath the
    weight of care?

164

Music, that knows no country, race or
   creed;
But gives to each according to his need.

UNKNOWN

Nature

Those gold candles fix'd in heaven's air.

WILLIAM SHAKESPEARE

When the oak is felled the whole forest
echoes with its fall, but a hundred acorns are
sown in silence by an unnoticed breeze.

THOMAS CARLYLE

AS A MAN SOWETH

We must not hope to be mowers,
   And to gather the ripe gold ears,
Unless we have first been sowers
   And watered the furrows with tears.

It is not just as we take it,
   This mystical world of ours,
Life's field will yield as we make it
   A harvest of thorns or of flowers.

JOHANN WOLFGANG VON GOETHE

Self-defense is nature's eldest law.

DRYDEN

Nothing happens to anybody which he is not fitted by nature to bear.

MARCUS AURELIUS ANTONINUS

It is a miserable thing to live in suspense, it is the life of the spider.

JONATHAN SWIFT

Let every bird sing its own note.

UNKNOWN

The stars hang bright above,
Silent, as if they watch'd the sleeping
    earth.

SAMUEL TAYLOR COLERIDGE

Night whose sable hand
Hangs on the purple skirts of flying day.

DYER

The winds blow from a thousand ways
    and waft their balms abroad,
The winds blow toward a million goals—
    but all winds blow from God.

SIR WALTER FOSS

O for a seat in some poetic nook,
Just hid with trees, and sparkling with
    a brook.

LEIGH HUNT

Night hath a thousand eyes.

JOHN LYLY

When you find that flowers and shrubs will not endure a certain atmosphere, it is a very significant hint to the human creature to remove out of that neighborhood.

MAYHEW

ROSES

Roses that briefly live,
  Joy is your dower—
Blest be the fates that give
  One perfect hour:—

And, though, too soon you die,
  In your dust glows
Something the passer-by
  Knows was a rose.

LOUISE CHANDLER MOULTON

The queen of night
Shines fair with all her virgin stars about her.

OTWAY

Open the casement, and up with the sun!
His gallant journey has now begun,
Over the hills his chariot is roll'd.
Banner'd with glory and burnish'd with gold;
Over the hills he comes sublime,
Bridegroom of earth, and brother of time!

MARTIN FARQUHAR TUPPER

Sweet, April showers
Do spring May flowers.

THOMAS TUSSER

He walks with Nature, and her paths are peace.

EDWARD YOUNG

The violet droops its soft and bashful brow,
But from its heart sweet incense fills the
air;—
So rich within—so pure without—art thou,
With modest mien and soul of virtue rare.

MRS. OSGOOD

Dashing in big drops on the narrow pane,
And making mournful music for the mind,
While plays his interlude the wizard wind,
I hear the singing of the frequent rain.

WILLIAM HENRY BURLEIGH

Wide flush the fields; the softening air is
balm;
Echo the mountains round; the forest smiles;
And every sense and every heart is joy.

THOMSON

Sail while the breeze blows, wind and tide wait for no man.

UNKNOWN

168

The glorious lamp of heaven, the sun.

HERRICK

'Tis distance lends enchantment to the view,
And robes the mountain in its azure hue.

THOMAS CAMPBELL

If winter comes, can spring be far behind?

PERCY BYSSHE SHELLEY

It is not growing like a tree
In bulk, doth make man better be;
Or standing long an oak, three hundred year,
To fall a log at last, dry, bald, and sear;
A lily of a day
Is fairer far, in May,
Although it fall and die that night,
It was a plant and flower of Light.
In small portions we just beauties see;
And in short measures life may perfect be.

BEN JONSON

Society is like a lawn where every roughness is smoothed, every bramble eradicated, and where the eye is delighted by the smiling verdure of a velvet surface. He, however, who would study nature in its wildness and variety, must plunge into the forest, must explore the glen, must stem the torrent, and dare the precipice.

WASHINGTON IRVING

May not taste be compared to that exquisite sense of the bee, which instantly discovers and extracts the quintessence of every flower, and disregards all the rest of it?

GREVILLE

Tears, idle tears, I know not what they
     mean,
Tears from the depth of some divine
     despair
Rise in the heart and gather in the eyes,
In looking on the happy autumn fields,
And thinking of the days that are no more.

ALFRED, LORD TENNYSON

Winter is on my head, but eternal spring is in my heart; I breathe at this hour the fragrance of the lilacs, the violets, and the roses, as at twenty years ago. The nearer I approach to the end, the plainer I hear around me the immortal symphonies of the worlds which invite me.

VICTOR HUGO

He who would gather roses must not fear thorns.

UNKNOWN

Traverse the desert, and then ye can tell
What treasures exist in the cold deep well,
Sink in despair on the red parch'd earth.
And then ye may reckon what water is worth.

ELIZA COOK

Our foster-nurse of nature is repose.

WILLIAM SHAKESPEARE

Nature fits all her children with something
     to do,

170

He who would write and can't write, can
   surely review.

JAMES RUSSELL LOWELL

Oh! nature's noblest gift—my grey goose quill:
Slave of my thoughts, obedient to my will,
Torn from thy parent bird to form a pen,
That mighty instrument of little men!

LORD BYRON

Flowers are like the pleasures of the world.

WILLIAM SHAKESPEARE

Crab apples may not be the best kind of fruit;
but a tree which every year bears a great crop
of crab apples is better worth cultivating than
a tree which bears nothing.

UNKNOWN

Kindred objects kindred thoughts inspire,
As summer clouds flash forth electric fire.

ROGERS

See the descending sun
Scatt'ring his beams about him as he sinks,
And gilding heaven above, and seas beneath,
With paint no mortal pencil can express.

HOPKINS

One touch of nature makes the whole world
kin.

WILLIAM SHAKESPEARE

All things are artificial, for nature is the art of God.

SIR THOMAS BROWNE

Nature, the vicar of the Almighty Lord.

GEOFFREY CHAUCER

Surely there is something in the unruffled calm of nature that owerawes our little anxieties and doubts: the sight of the deep-blue sky and the clustering stars above, seem to impart a quiet to the mind.

JONATHAN EDWARDS

To him who in the love of Nature holds
Communion with her visible forms, she
  speaks
A various language.

WILLIAM CULLEN BRYANT

How beautiful is the rain!
After the dust and heat,
In the broad and fiery street,
In the narrow lane;
How beautiful is the rain!
How it clatters along the roofs,
Like the tramp of hoofs;
How it gushes and struggles out
From the throat of the overflowing spout.

HENRY WADSWORTH LONGFELLOW

The lofty pine is oftenest agitated by the wind—high towers rush to the earth with a heavier fall—and the lightning most frequently strikes the highest mountains.

HORACE

THE RAINY DAY

The day is cold and dark and dreary;
It rains, and the wind is never weary;
The vine still clings to the moldering wall,
But at every gust the dead leaves fall.
  And the day is dark and dreary.

My life is cold and dark and dreary;
It rains and the wind is never weary;
My thoughts still cling to the moldering past,
But the hopes of youth fall thick in the
    blast,
  And the days are dark and dreary.

Be still, sad heart! and cease repining;
Behind the clouds is the sun still shining;
Thy fate is the common fate of all:
Into each life some rain must fall,
  Some days must be dark and dreary.

HENRY WADSWORTH LONGFELLOW

Midsummer madness.

WILLIAM SHAKESPEARE

Water, water, everywhere,
Nor any drop to drink.

SAMUEL TAYLOR COLERIDGE

There are two worlds: the world that we can measure with line and rule, and the world that

173

we feel with our hearts and imagination.

LEIGH HUNT

It seems that nature has concealed at the bottom of our minds, talents and abilities of which we are not aware. The passions alone have the privilege of bringing them to light, and of giving us sometimes view more certain and more perfect than art could possibly produce.

DUC DE LA ROCHEFOUCAULD

There they stand, the innumerable stars,
Shining in order like a living hymn,
Written in light.

NATHANIEL PARKER WILLIS

They could neither of 'em speak for rage and so fell a sputtering at one another like two roasting apples.

WILLIAM CONGREVE

The old oaken bucket, the iron-bound
    bucket,
The moss-covered bucket which hung in
    the well.

SAMUEL WOODWORTH

One swallow does not make a summer.

ARISTOTLE

Peace

We must take the nations of the world as they are, the human passions and prejudices of peoples as they exist, and find some way to secure . . . a peaceful world.

GEORGE CATLETT MARSHALL

Down the dark future, through long
    generations,
The echoing sounds grow fainter and then
    cease;
And like a bell, with solemn, sweet vibrations,
I hear once more the voice of Christ say
    "Peace!"

HENRY WADSWORTH LONGFELLOW

Blessed are the peacemakers: for they shall be called the children of God.

ST. MATTHEW v. 9

Blessed is the peacemaker, not the conqueror.

UNKNOWN

Drop thy still dew of quietness,
    Till all our strivings cease;
Take from our souls the strain and stress,
And let our ordered lives confess
    The beauty of Thy peace.

JOHN GREENLEAF WHITTIER

Peace was the first thing the Angels sang.
Peace is the mark of the sons of God. Peace is
the nurse of love. Peace is the mother of unity.
Peace is the rest of blessed souls. Peace is the
dwelling place for eternity.

LEO THE GREAT

A crust eaten in peace is better than a
banquet partaken in anxiety.

AESOP

Thou mayst hold a serpent by the
    tongue,
A chafed lion by the mortal paw,
A fasting tiger safer by the tooth,
Than keep in peace that hand which thou
    dost hold.

WILLIAM SHAKESPEARE

O liberty! O liberty! What crimes are com-
mitted in thy name!

JEANNE MANON ROLAND

Peace hath her victories,
No less renown'd than war.

JOHN MILTON

Poverty

It is not easy for men to rise whose qualities
are thwarted by poverty.

JUVENAL

Beggars should be no choosers.

JOHN HEYWOOD

When poverty comes in at the door, love flies
out the window.

ANON.

To mortal men great loads allotted be;
But of all packs no pack like poverty.

HERRICK

Some for renown, on scraps of learning dote,
And think they grow immortal as they quote.
To patchwork learn'd quotations are allied,
But strive to make our poverty our pride.

EDWARD YOUNG

Poverty makes people satirical,—soberly,
sadly, bitterly satirical.

FRISWELL

Take care to be an economist in prosperity; there is no fear of your not being one in adversity.

JOHANN G. ZIMMERMAN

Want of prudence is too frequently the want of virtue; nor is there on earth a more powerful advocate for vice than poverty.

OLIVER GOLDSMITH

Neither great poverty, nor great riches, will hear reason.

HENRY FIELDING

The lack of wealth is easily repaired; but the poverty of the soul is irreparable.

MONTAIGNE

Adversity's sweet milk, philosophy.

WILLIAM SHAKESPEARE

Adversity has the effect of eliciting talents, which in prosperous circumstances would have lain dormant.

HORACE

It is not poverty so much as pretence that harasses a ruined man—the struggle between a proud mind and an empty purse—the keeping up a hollow show that must soon come to an end. Have the courage to appear poor, and you disarm poverty to its sharpest sting.

ANNA JAMESON

Sloth makes all things difficult, but industry all easy; and he that riseth late, must trot all day, and shall scarce overtake his business at night; while laziness travels so slowly, that poverty soon overtakes him.

BENJAMIN FRANKLIN

A light purse makes a heavy heart.

UNKNOWN

Frugality may be termed the daughter of prudence, the sister of temperance, and the parent of liberty. He that is extravagant will quickly become poor, and poverty will enforce dependence and invite corruption.

SAMUEL JOHNSON

Prayer

I do not ask for any crown
  But that which all may win;
Nor try to conquer any world
  Except the one within.
Be Thou my guide until I find
  Led by a tender hand,
The happy kingdom in myself
  And dare to take command.

LOUISA MAY ALCOTT

Act upon your impulses, but pray that they may be directed by God.

EMERSON TENNENT

I NEVER THOUGHT TO
OFFER THANKS

I've always said my daily prayers
For I thought that I should pray.
And so I learned the routine ones
And said them every day.

They were the ones that someone else
Had written long ago
So they were never quite my own;
But how was I to know

Just what to say to God that would
Explain to Him my needs
When I had everything I wanted?
I never thought of it as greed

To ask for more and more of life;
For fortune and for great success
With all about me friends to make
And share my happiness.

And so for all the wealth of life—
The kind not stored in banks—
For just the breath I drew each day,
I never thought to offer thanks.

But now it seems as I grow wiser
With the coming of each day
And I am substituting "Thanks" for "Please"
When it's time for me to pray.

ELIZABETH SMITH

Prayer purifies; it is a self-preached sermon.

RICHTER

Fountain of mercy! whose pervading eye
Can look within and read what passes there,

180

*Accept my thoughts for thanks; I have no
    words.
My soul o'erfraught with gratitude, rejects
The aid of language—Lord!—behold my
    heart.*

HANNAH MORE

O Lord, forgive us for being so sensitive about the things that do not matter—and so insensitive to the things that do! Amen.

UNKNOWN

*O grant me, heav'n, a middle state
Neither too humble or too great;
More than enough for nature's ends,
With something left to treat my friends.*

MALLET

Thank God every morning when you get up that you have something to do which must be done, whether you like it or not. Being forced to work, and forced to do your best, will breed in you temperance, self-control, diligence, strength of will, content, and a hundred other virtues which the idle never know.

CHARLES KINGSLEY

Let prayer be the key of the morning and the bolt of the evening.

MATHEW HENRY

We should act with as much energy as those who expect everything from themselves; and we should pray with as much earnestness as those who expect everything from God.

CHARLES CALEB COLTON

God, give me sympathy and sense,
  And help me keep my courage high;
God, give me calm and confidence,
  And—please—a twinkle in my eye.
  Amen.

MARGARET BAILEY

Any heart turned Godward, feels more
    joy
In one short hour of prayer, than e'er was
    rais'd
By all the feasts on earth since its
    foundation.

GAMALIEL BAILEY

THESE THINGS I HAVE

I wanted health and strength to do great
    things,
Infirmity taught patience for each day.
My strength, as fleeting as a moth's white
    wing,
Lift me dependent, that I might obey.
I wanted wealth for happiness and ease,
But poverty prevailed and made me wise.
I wanted power to conquer and to please,
But weakness made me see through others'
    eyes.
I wanted leisure time to dream and plan,
But duty brought self-discipline and while
I sought approval of my fellowman,
I found it not, but in my Savior's smile.
And now that I have been so richly blest,
This is my daily prayer, "Give what is best."

JOSEPHINE STONE BREEDING

Ye ask, and receive not, because ye ask amiss.

JAMES iv, 3

If any of you lack wisdom, let him ask of God, that giveth to all men liberally and upbraideth not; and it shall be given him. But let him ask in faith, nothing wavering.

JAMES i, 5, 6

More things are wrought by prayer
Than this world dreams of.

ALFRED, LORD TENNYSON

In prayer it is better to have a heart without words, than words without a heart.

JOHN BUNYAN

Is not prayer a study of truth—a sally of the soul into the unfound infinite? No man ever prayed heartily without learning something; but when a faithful thinker resolute to detach every object from personal relations, and see it in the light of thought, shall, at the same time, kindle science with the fire of the holiest affections, then with God go forth anew into the creation.

RALPH WALDO EMERSON

Give us grace and strength to persevere. Give us courage and gaiety and the quiet mind. Spare us to our friends and soften us to our enemies. Give us the strength to encounter that which is to come, that we may be brave in peril, constant in tribulation, temperate in wrath and in all changes of fortune, and down to the gates of death loyal and loving to one another.

ROBERT LOUIS STEVENSON

Swift to its close ebbs out life's little day;
Earth's joys grow dim, its glories pass way;
Change and decay in all around I see:
O thou who changeth not, abide with me!

JOHN KEBLE

FROM "THE FORCE OF PRAYER"

Oh! there is never sorrow of heart
That shall lack a timely end,
If but to God we turn, and ask
Of Him to be our friend!

WILLIAM WORDSWORTH

'Mid all the traffic of the ways—
Turmoils without, within—
Make in my heart a quiet place,
And come and dwell therein;

A little place of mystic grace,
Of self and sin swept bare,
Where I may look upon thy face,
And talk with thee in prayer.

UNKNOWN

STEADFAST HEART

I've dreamed many dreams that never
    came true.
I've seen them vanish at dawn,
But I've realized enough of my dreams,
    Thank God,
To make me want to dream on.

I've prayed many prayers when no answer
    came,

Though I waited patient and long,
But answers have come to enough of my
    prayers
To make me keep praying on.

I've trusted many a friend that failed,
And left me to weep alone,
But I've found enough of my friends true
    blue,
To make me keep trusting on.

I've sown many seed that fell by the way
For the birds to feed upon,
But I've held enough golden sheaves in my
    hands
To make me keep sowing on.

I've drained the cup of disappointment and
    pain
And gone many ways without song,
But I've sipped enough nectar from the
    roses of life
To make me want to live on.

UNKNOWN

MORNING PRAYER

When little things would irk me, and I
    grow
Impatient with my dear ones, make me
    know
How in a moment joy can take its flight
And happiness be quenched in endless
    night.
Keep this thought with me all the livelong
    day
That I may guard the harsh words I might
    say

When I would fret and grumble fiery hot,
.At trifles that tomorrow are forgot—
Let me remember, Lord, how it would be
If these, my loved ones, were not here
    with me.

UNKNOWN

Procrastination

A finger in every pie.

MIGUEL DE CERVANTES

The day I did not sweep the house there came
to it one I did not expect.

UNKNOWN

Often the precious present is wasted in
visions of the future.

MARTIN FARQUHAR TUPPER

Defer not till tomorrow to be wise,
Tomorrow's sun to thee may never rise.

WILLIAM CONGREVE

Never put off till to-morrow what you can
    do today.

Never trouble another for what you can
   do yourself.
Never spend your money before you have
   it.
Never buy what you do not want because
   it is cheap.
Pride costs us more than hunger, thirst,
   and cold.
We seldom repent having eaten too little.
Nothing is troublesome that we do willingly.
How much pain the evils have cost us that
   have never happened!
Take things always by the smooth handle.
When angry, count ten before you speak:
   if very angry, a hundred.

THOMAS JEFFERSON

To-morrow cheats us all. Why dost thou
   stay,
And leave undone what should be done
   to-day?
Begin—the present minute's in thy power;
But still t' adjourn, and wait a fitter hour,
Is like the clown, who at some river's side
Expecting stands, in hopes the running
   tide
Will all ere long be past. Fool! not to know
It still has flow'd the same, and will
   forever flow.

HUGHES

Strength for to-day is all we need,
   For there never will be a to-morrow;
For to-morrow will prove but another to-day
   With its measure of joy and of sorrow.

UNKNOWN

One of these days is none of these days.

UNKNOWN

187

Procrastination is the thief of time.

EDWARD YOUNG

GOOD IMPULSES

It isn't the thing you do;
It's the thing you leave undone,
Which gives you a bit of heartache
At the setting of the sun.
The tender word forgotten,
The letter you did not write,
The flower you might have sent,
Are your haunting ghosts at night.

MARGARET ELIZABETH SANGSTER

What may be done at any time will be done at no time.

UNKNOWN

Proverbs

A good name is a sound inheritance.

UNKNOWN

It is hard for an empty bag to stand upright.

BENJAMIN FRANKLIN

Light is the task when many share the toil.

HOMER

You can never have a greater or a less dominion than that over yourself.

LEONARDO DA VINCI

Who serves his country well has no need of ancestors.

VOLTAIRE

Comparisons are odious.

JOHN FORTESCUE

No man can lose what he never had.

IZAAK WALTON

Hell is truth seen too late.

HENRY GARDINER ADAMS

Maxims are the condensed good sense of nations.

SIR JAMES MACKINTOSH

Letters which are warmly sealed are often but coldly opened.

RICHTER

He hath eaten me out of house and home.

WILLIAM SHAKESPEARE

He kept him as the apple of his eye.

DEUT. xxxii, 10.

Charity shall cover a multitude of sins.

PETER iv, 8.

Praise was originally a pension, paid by the world.

SWIFT

It makes us, or mars us.

WILLIAM SHAKESPEARE

A picture is a poem without words.

HORACE

A good name is rather to be chosen than great riches; and loving favor rather than silver and gold.

SOLOMON

Blessed are they that have not seen, and yet have believed.

JESUS CHRIST

Blessed are the meek: for they shall inherit the earth.

JESUS CHRIST

He jests at scars, that never felt a wound.

WILLIAM SHAKESPEARE

The child is father of the man.

WILLIAM WORDSWORTH

Fools rush in where angels fear to tread.

ALEXANDER POPE

Bad excuses are worse than none.

UNKNOWN

A man who does nothing never has time to do anything.

UNKNOWN

This was the noblest Roman of them all.

WILLIAM SHAKESPEARE

The coast was clear.

MICHAEL DRAYTON

The pot calls the kettle black.

MIGUEL DE CERVANTES

Thank you for nothing.

MIGUEL DE CERVANTES

The parent's life is the child's copy-book.

W. S. PARTRIDGE

Not worth his salt.

PETRONIUS

A horse! a horse! my kingdom for a horse!

WILLIAM SHAKESPEARE

Mum's the word.

MIGUEL DE CERVANTES

'Mean to' don't pick no cotton.

UNKNOWN

A half-truth is a whole lie.

HEBREW PROVERB

Out of the frying pan into the fire.

TERTULLIAN

The rotten apple injures his neighbor.

UNKNOWN

The day is for honest men, the night for thieves.

EURIPIDES

What is not good for the swarm is not good for the bee.

MARCUS AURELIUS ANTONINUS

A rolling stone gathers no moss.

PUBLIUS SYRUS

Fish and visitors smell in three days.

BENJAMIN FRANKLIN

He that lies with the dogs, riseth with fleas.

GEORGE HERBERT

Every dog must have his day.

SWIFT

I call a fig a fig, a spade a spade.

MENANDER

A great flame follows a little spark.

DANTE ALIGHIERI

Birds of a feather flock together.

GEORGE WITHER

The eye is bigger than the belly.

GEORGE HERBERT

Mud thrown is ground lost.

UNKNOWN

Conceal a flaw, and the world will imagine
the worst.

MARTIAL

In all abundance there is lack.

HIPPOCRATES

A good dinner sharpens wit, while it softens the heart.

JOHN DORAN

The empty vessel makes the greatest sound.

WILLIAM SHAKESPEARE

All feet cannot wear one shoe.

UNKNOWN

It takes two to make a quarrel.

UNKNOWN

As quiet as a lamb.

WILLIAM SHAKESPEARE

As cold as cucumbers.

BEAUMONT AND FLETCHER

It is not only fine feathers that make fine birds.

AESOP

A cat is a lion to the mouse.

ALBANIAN

Home is where the heart is.

PLINY

Many have fallen by the edge of the sword,
but not so many as have fallen by the tongue.

ECCLESIASTES

Maybe ain't ain't so correct, but I notice that
lots of folks who ain't using ain't ain't eatin'.

WILL ROGERS

Children have more need of models than of
critics.

JOSEPH JOUBERT

You get what you pay for.

GABRIEL BIEL

A bad beginning makes a bad ending.

EURIPIDES

Not every word requires an answer.

UNKNOWN

Talk does not cook rice.

CHINESE PROVERB

All things whatsoever ye would that men
should do unto you, do ye even so to them.

MATT. vii, 12

One picture is worth more than ten thousand
words.

CHINESE PROVERB

If I had not lifted up the stone, you had not found the jewel.

HEBREW PROVERB

He who does not honor his wife dishonors himself.

SPANISH PROVERB

Those who bestow too much application on trifling things, become generally incapable of great ones.

DUC DE LA ROCHEFOUCAULD

He that spareth his rod hateth his son.

PROVERBS xiii, 24

There is no accounting for tastes.

LATIN PROVERB

This hitteth the nail on the head.

JOHN HEYWOOD

Let the buyer beware.

LATIN PROVERB

Hell is paved with good intentions.

JOHN RAY

Necessity is the mother of invention.

ANON. LATIN SAYING

It is a true proverb, that if you live with a lame man you will learn to limp.

PLUTARCH

You cannot prevent the birds of sorrow from flying over your head, but you can prevent them from building nests in your hair.

CHINESE PROVERB

New brooms sweep well.

FREIDANK

I know on which side my bread is buttered.

JOHN HEYWOOD

Many hands make light work.

JOHN HEYWOOD

The more the merrier.

JOHN HEYWOOD

He that is slow to anger is better than the mighty; and he that ruleth his spirit than he that taketh a city.

PROVERBS 16:32

Actions speak louder than words.

ANCIENT PROVERB

My Son, if sinners entice thee, consent thou not.

PROVERBS 1:10

An ounce of prevention is worth a pound of cure.

ENGLISH PROVERB

Let another man praise thee, and not thine own mouth; a stranger, and not thine own lips.

PROVERBS xxvii, 2.

Train up a child in the way he should go; and when he is old, he will not depart from it.

PROVERBS xxii, 6

A handsome shoe often pinches the foot.

UNKNOWN

The wheel of fortune turns incessantly round, and who can say within himself, I shall to-day be uppermost.

CONFUCIUS

It did me yeoman's service.

WILLIAM SHAKESPEARE

All Gaul is divided in three parts.

JULIUS CAESAR

You cannot teach a crab to walk straight.

ARISTOPHANES

Barkis is willin'.

CHARLES DICKENS

You also, Brutus my son.

JULIUS CAESAR

You may go whistle for the rest.

MIGUEL DE CERVANTES

Religion

That "God is love" is not one side of the truth, but the whole truth about God—there is no other side.

REV. J. M. GIBBON

Pardon, I beseech Thee, the iniquity of this people, according unto the greatness of Thy mercy . . . And the Lord said, I have pardoned, according to thy word.

NUMBERS, xiv, 19

Thou art a God ready to pardon, gracious and merciful, slow to anger, and of great kindness.

NEHEMIAH ix, 17

Suffer the little children, and forbid them not to come unto me; for of such is the kingdom of Heaven.

JESUS CHRIST

An atheist is but a mad ridiculous derider of piety; but a hypocrite makes a sober jest of God and religion; he finds it easier to be upon his knees than to rise to a good action.

ALEXANDER POPE

Atheism is rather in the life than in the heart of man.

FRANCIS BACON

It would be well, if some who have taken upon themselves the ministry of the Gospel, that they would first preach to themselves, then afterwards to others.

CARDINAL POLE

There is an Eye that never sleeps
  Beneath the wing of night;
There is an Ear that never shuts
  When sink the beams of light.

There is an Arm that never tires
  When human strength gives way;
There is a Love that never fails
  When earthly loves decay.

That Eye is fix'd on seraph throngs:
That Ear is fill'd with angel's songs;
That Arm upholds the worlds on high;
That Love is thron'd beyond the sky.

HEBER

FROM "L'ENVOI"

When earth's last picture is painted, and the
    tubes are twisted and dried,
When the oldest colors have faded, and the
    youngest critic has died,
We shall rest, and, faith, we shall need it—
    lie down for an eon or two,
Till the Master of All Good Workmen shall
    set us to work anew!

And those that were good shall be happy:
    they shall sit in a golden chair;
They shall splash at a ten-league canvas
    with brushes of comet's hair;
They shall find real saints to draw from—
    Magdalene, Peter, and Paul;
They shall work for an age at a sitting and
    never be tired at all!

And only the Master shall praise us, and
    only the Master shall blame;
And no one shall work for money, and no
    one shall work for fame;
But each for the joy of the working, and
    each, in his separate star
Shall draw the Thing as he sees it for The
    God of Things as They Are.

RUDYARD KIPLING

FATHER, THY WILL BE DONE

He sendeth sun, He sendeth shower,
Alike they are needful for the flower;

And joys and tears alike are sent
To give the soul fit nourishment:
   As comes to me or cloud or sun,
   Father, Thy will, not mine, be done!

SARAH FLOWER ADAMS

He leads the humble in what is right,
And teaches the humble his way.

PSALMS 25:9

Remember the week day, and keep it holy too.

UNKNOWN

THANK GOD

   Thank God for life!
E'en though it bring much bitterness and
    strife,
   And all our fairest hopes be wrecked
    and lost,
E'en though there be more ill than good
    in life,
   We cling to life and reckon not the cost.
   Thank God for life!

   Thank God for love!
For though sometimes grief follows in its
    wake,
   Still we forget love's sorrow in love's joy,
And cherish tears with smiles for love's
    dear sake;
   Only in heaven is bliss without alloy.
   Thank God for love!

Thank God for pain!
No tear hath ever yet been shed in vain,
    And in the end each sorrowing heart shall
        find
No curse, but blessings in the hand of pain;
    Even when he smiteth, then is God
        most kind,
    Thank God for pain!

Thank God for death!
Who touches anguished lips and stills their
        breath
    And giveth peace unto each troubled
        breast;
Grief flows before thy touch, O blessed
        death;
    God's sweetest gift, thy name in heaven
        is Rest.
    Thank God for death!

UNKNOWN

Heaven—it is God's throne. The earth—it is
his footstool.

MATTHEW v, 34

He knows, He loves, He cares;
    Nothing this truth can dim.
He gives the very best to those
    Who leave the choice with Him.

UNKNOWN

Order is heaven's first law.

MILTON

What is God? Everything.

PINDAR

The life of a pious minister is visible rhetoric.

HERMAN HOOKER

The Sabbath was made for man, and not man for the Sabbath.

ST. MARK ii, 27

Alas! while the body stands so broad and brawny, must the soul lie blinded, dwarfed, stupefied, almost annihilated? Alas! this was, too, a breath of God, bestowed in heaven, but on earth never to be unfolded!

CARLYLE

One can never repeat too often, that reason, as it exists in man, is only our intellectual eye, and that, like the eye, to see, it needs light,—to see clearly and far, it needs the light of heaven.

ANON.

Worship as if thou wert to die today.

TUSCAN

Religion is the best armor that a man can have, but it is the worst cloak.

BUNYAN

Genuine religion is not so much a matter of feeling as of principle.

ANON.

It is the Lord: let Him do what seemeth Him good.

I SAMUEL, iii, 18

A little philosophy inclineth man's mind to atheism, but depth in philosophy bringeth men's mind about to religion.

FRANCIS BACON

A man devoid of religion, is like a horse without a bridle.

FROM THE LATIN

Let never day nor night unhallow'd pass,
But still remember what the Lord has done.

WILLIAM SHAKESPEARE

For in religion as in friendship, they who profess most are ever the least sincere.

SHERIDAN

The Lord gave, and the Lord hath taken away; blessed be the name of the Lord.

JOB i, 21

Who don't keep faith with God won't keep it with man.

UNKNOWN

God moves in a mysterious way
His wonders to perform;
He plants His footsteps in the sea
And rides upon the storm.

WILLIAM COWPER

Sunday is the golden clasp that binds together the volume of the week.

HENRY WADSWORTH LONGFELLOW

Religion is meant to be bread for daily use, not cake for special occasions.

UNKNOWN

*Who in or out, who moves the grand
    machine,
Nor stirs my curiosity, or spleen;
Secrets of state no more I wish to know
Than secret movements of a puppet-show;
Let but the puppets move, I've my desire,
Unseen the hand which guides the master
    wire.*

CHURCHILL

A world without a Sabbath would be like a man without a smile, like a summer without flowers, and like a homestead without a garden. It is the joyous day of the whole week.

HENRY WARD BEECHER

No atheist, as such, can be a true friend, an affectionate relation, or a loyal subject.

DR. BENTLEY

Atheism is the result of ignorance and pride; of strong sense and feeble reasons; of good eating and ill-living. It is the plague of society, the corrupter of manners, and the underminer of property.

JEREMY COLLIER

The ways of heaven are dark and intricate,
Puzzled in mazes, and perplex'd with errors;
Our understanding traces them in vain,
Lost and bewilder'd in the fruitless search;
Nor sees with how much art the windings run,
Nor where the regular confusion ends.

ADDISON

Men will wrangle for religion; write for it;
fight for it; die for it; anything but—*live for it.*

CHARLES CALEB COLTON

Repentance,
A salve, a comfort, and a cordial;
He that hath her, the keys of heaven hath:
This is the guide, this is the post, the path.

DRAYTON

I have lived long enough to know what I did
not at one time believe—that no society can be
upheld in happiness and honor without the
sentiment of religion.

PIERRE SIMON DE LAPLACE

Of right and wrong he taught
Truths as refined as ever Athens heard;
And (strange to tell!) he practised what he
     preach'd.

ARMSTRONG

Heaven deigns to suit our trials to our
strength.

HANNAH MORE

How calmly may we commit ourselves to the hands of Him who bears up the world—of Him who has created, and who provides for the joy even of insects, as carefully as if He were their Father!

RICHTER

By night an atheist half believes a God.

YOUNG

Praise God, from whom all blessings flow!
Praise Him, all creatures here below!
Praise Him above, ye heavenly Host!
Praise Father, Son, and Holy Ghost!

BISHOP THOMAS KEN

The minister is to be a live man, a real man, a true man, a simple man, great in his love, great in his life, great in his work, great in his simplicity, great in his gentleness.

JOHN HALL

Whate'er my doom;
It cannot be unhappy: God hath given me
The boon of resignation.

DANIEL WILSON

God is a spirit; and they that worship Him, must worship Him in spirit and in truth.

ST. JOHN iv, 24

He that cometh to God, must believe that He is, and that He is a rewarder of them that diligently seek Him.

HEB. xi, 6

Pure religion and undefiled before God and the Father is this: To visit the fatherless and widows in their affliction, and to keep himself unspotted from the world.

JAMES i, 27

Blessed are they that hear the word of God, and keep it.

ISAIAH

One loves God only through knowledge, and the degree of love corresponds to the degree of knowledge.

MAIMONIDES

CONSOLATION

He knows, He loves, He cares;
  Nothing this truth can dim.
He gives the very best to those
  Who leave the choice to him.

UNKNOWN

Sophisticated, wordly-wise,
I searched for God and found Him not,
Until one day, the world forgot,
I found Him in my baby's eyes.

MARY AFTON THACKER

Trust no Future, howe'er pleasant!
Let the dead Past bury its dead!

Act—act in the living present!
Heart within, and God o'erhead!

HENRY WADSWORTH LONGFELLOW

In this vast universe
There is but one supreme truth—
That God is our friend!
By that truth meaning is given
To the remote stars, the numberless centuries,
The long and heroic struggle of mankind . . .
O my Soul, dare to trust this truth!
Dare to rest in God's kindly arms,
Dare to look confidently into His face,
Then launch thyself into life unafraid!
Knowing thou art within thy Father's house,
That thou art surrounded by His love,
Thou wilt become master of fear,
Lord of life, conqueror even of death!

UNKNOWN

Success

THE WAY TO POWER

Self-reverence, self-knowledge, self-control,
These three alone lead life to sovereign
    power.
Yet not for power (power of herself
Would come uncall'd for) but to live by law,
Acting the law we live by without fear;
And, because right is right, to follow right
Were wisdom in the scorn of consequence.

ALFRED, LORD TENNYSON

O what a glory doth this world put on,
For him who with fervent heart goes forth,
Under the bright and glorious sky and looks
On duties well performed, and days well
  spent.

HENRY WADSWORTH LONGFELLOW

THE BLESSINGS OF WORK

If you wake up in the morning
  With your hardest job to do,
Don't start the day with grumbling—
  That won't help you see it through.
Be glad for work that's difficult,
  For tasks that challenge you!
Workers find a thousand blessings
  The idle never knew.

UNKNOWN

The greatest achievement of the human spirit is to live up to one's opportunities and make the most of one's resources.

MARQUIS DE VAUVENARGUES

Try not to become a man of success but rather try to become a man of value.

ALBERT EINSTEIN

The Margin of Success: Make good! Don't complain! Do the things you are expected to do—and more. Don't waste time in giving reasons why you didn't, or couldn't, or wouldn't. The less you do, the more you complain. Efficiency—keep that word in your heart. Get to saying that word in your sleep. Do your work a little better than anyone else does it. That is the margin of success.

UNKNOWN

RECIPE FOR SUCCESS

Bite off more than you can chew,
Then chew it.
Plan more than you can do,
Then do it.
Point your arrow at a star,
Take your aim, and there you are.

Arrange more time than you can spare,
Then spare it.
Take on more than you can bear,
Then bear it.
Plan your castle in the air,
Then build a ship to take you there.

UNKNOWN

Defeat is not bitter if you don't swallow it.

UNKNOWN

The cautious seldom err.

CONFUCIUS

Whatever is worth doing at all, is worth doing well.

EARL OF CHESTERFIELD

The surest way not to fail is to determine to succeed.

RICHARD BRINSLEY SHERIDAN

You never know what you can do till you try.

A. MACLAREN, D.D.

Success doesn't come to those who wait—
and it doesn't wait for anyone to come to it.

UNKNOWN

The men who try to do something and fail are
infinitely better than those who try to do
nothing and succeed.

LLOYD JONES

Men were born to succeed, not to fail.

HENRY DAVID THOREAU

I have learned that success is to be measured
not so much by the position that one has
reached in life as by the obstacles which he has
overcome while trying to succeed.

BOOKER T. WASHINGTON

Ideals are like stars; you will not succeed in
touching them with your hands. But like the
seafaring man on the desert of waters, you
choose them as your guides, and following
them you reach your destiny.

CARL SCHURZ

It is success that colors all in life;
Success makes fools admir'd, makes villains
*   honest:*
All the proud virtue of this vaunting world
Fawns on success and power, howe'er
*   acquired.*

JAMES THOMSON

It is a rough road that leads to the heights of greatness.

SENECA

What we ardently wish we soon believe.

OWEN D. YOUNG

There is always another chance .... This thing that we call "failure" is not the falling down, but the staying down.

MARY PICKFORD

A slave has but one master; the ambitious man has as many masters as there are persons whose aid may contribute to the advancement of his fortune.

JEAN DE LA BRUYERE

There are in business three things necessary—knowledge, temper and time.

FELTHAM

In the gates of Eternity, the black hand and the white hand hold each other with an equal clasp.

HARRIET BEECHER STOWE

WISDOM IN A PHRASE

When President Eliot, of Harvard, was asked how he accounted for his good health and vigorous mind at his advanced age (he was then 88, and lived 8 years longer) he included in his reply this significant phrase:

"A calm temperament expectant of good."

Here is a phrase of only six words, but one of concentrated wisdom. Others have expressed the same idea differently but none so felicitously as did Harvard's famous president. This phrase is an inclusive definition of optimism, for the optimist calmly looks on the bright side of things, and the bright side is expected to bring forth good.

To be sure, a calm temperament is denied to many, and it is difficult to acquire, but anyone, if he choose, can live his daily life "expectant of good."

Dr. Eliot clothed an old idea in new words, and the more they are pondered the more effective they appear, the more worth while to be stored in one's mind. Old age cannot be prevented, but its unpleasant mental manifestations may be retarded to a degree, without doubt, by "a calm temperament expectant of good."

UNKNOWN

ASPIRATION

Let me but live my life from year to year,
  With forward face and unreluctant soul;
  Not hurrying to, nor returning from, the
    goal;
Not mourning for the things that disappear
In the dim past, nor holding back in fear
  From what the future veils; but with a
    whole

215

And happy heart, that pays its toll
To Youth and Age, and travels on with cheer.

So let the way wind up the hill or down,
  O'er rough or smooth, the journey will
    be joy:
  Still seeking what I sought when but a
    boy,
New friendship, high adventure, and a
    crown,
  My heart will keep the courage of the
    quest,
  And hope the road's last turn will be
    the best.

HENRY VAN DYKE

Whoso neglects learning in his youth,
Loses the past and is dead for the future.

EURIPIDES

There are souls which fall from heaven
like flowers, but ere they bloom are crushed
under the foul tread of some brutal hoof.

JEAN PAUL RICHTER

Some day the silver cord will break,
  And I no more as now shall sing;
But oh, the joy when I shall wake
  Within the palace of the King!
And I shall see him face to face . . .

UNKNOWN

Time

Midnight,—strange mystic hour,—when the veil between the frail present and the eternal future grows thin.

HARRIET BEECHER STOWE

Who shall contend with time, unvanquished
    time,
The conqueror of conquerors, and lord of
    desolation?

KIRK WHITE

Still on it creeps,
Each little moment at another's heels,
Till hours, days, years, and ages are made
    up
Of such small parts as these, and men look
    back
Worn and bewildered, wondering how it is.
Thou trav'llest like a ship in the wide ocean,
Which hath no bounding shore to mark its
    progress.

JOANNA BAILLIE

Time wasted is existence; us'd is life.

EDWARD YOUNG

Time is the chrysalis of eternity.

JOHANN PAUL FRIEDRICH RICHTER

HOW TROUBLESOME IS DAY

How troublesome is day!
It calls us from our sleep away;
It bids us from our pleasant dreams awake,
It sends us forth to keep or break
Our promises to pay.

THOMAS LOVE PEACOCK

Better late than never.

LIVY

Gather ye rosebuds while ye may.
  Old Time is still a-flying,
And this same flower that smiles today,
  Tomorrow will be dying.

ROBERT HERRICK

Time, as he passes us, has a dove's wing,
Unsoil'd and swift, and of a silken sound.

COWPER

To-day is ours: why do we fear?
To-day is ours: we have it here;
Let's banish bus'ness, banish sorrow:
To the gods belongs to-morrow.

COWLEY

The goal of yesterday will be the starting point of tomorrow.

CARLYLE

You may have time again, but not the time.

SIR R. BAKER

A day, an hour, of virtuous liberty
Is worth a whole eternity in bondage.

JOSEPH ADDISON

The inaudible and noiseless foot of time.

WILLIAM SHAKESPEARE

All that time is lost which might be better employed.

JEAN JACQUES ROUSSEAU

Now is now-here, but to-morrow's no-where.

UNKNOWN

Nothing is more precious than time, yet nothing less valued.

UNKNOWN

Winged time glides on insensibly, and deceives us; and there is nothing more fleeting than years.

OVID

This time like all other times is a very good one, if we but know what to do with it.

RALPH WALDO EMERSON

It is not the early rising, but the well spending of the day.

UNKNOWN

Dost thou love Life? Then do not squander Time; for that's the stuff Life is made of.

BENJAMIN FRANKLIN

As every thread of gold is valuable, so is every minute of time.

JOHN MASON

Time is the old Justice, that examines all offenders.

WILLIAM SHAKESPEARE

And thus the whirligig of time brings in his revenges.

WILLIAM SHAKESPEARE

There are two things to which we never grow accustomed—the ravages of time and the injustice of our fellow-men.

TALLEYRAND

Time cancels young pain.

EURIPIDES

It is thrifty to prepare today for the wants of tomorrow.

AESOP

Enjoy yourself. It is later than you think.

CHINESE PROVERB

The years as they pass plunder us of one thing after another.

HORACE

Time bears away all things, even our minds.

VIRGIL

FROM "THE OLD CLOCK"

Through days of sorrow and of mirth,
Through days of death and days of birth.
Through every swift vicissitude
Of changeful time, unchanged it has stood.
And as if, like God, it all things saw,
It calmly repeats those words of awe—

221

"Forever—never!
Never—forever!"

HENRY WADSWORTH LONGFELLOW

Hours are golden links;—God's tokens reaching heaven.

CHARLES DICKENS

One to-day is worth two to-morrows.

UNKNOWN

There is a past which is gone for ever; but there is a future which is still our own.

UNKNOWN

We waste, not use our time: we breathe, not live.

UNKNOWN

Lost time is never found again.

BENJAMIN FRANKLIN

He was not of an age but for all time.

BEN JONSON

Beware the ides of March.

WILLIAM SHAKESPEARE

Thirty days hath November,
April, June, and September,
February hath twenty-eight alone,
And all the rest have thirty-one.

RICHARD GRAFTON

History is the witness that testifies to the passing of time.

CICERO

Time is flying never to return.

VIRGIL

I was promised on a time
To have reason for my rhyme;
From that time until this season,
I received nor rhyme nor reason.

EDMUND SPENSER

The day is always his who works in it with serenity and great aims.

RALPH WALDO EMERSON

TIME

So the sands of Time that slowly flow
  From out my hour glass
Will all too soon have ebbed away,
  My life will then be past.
So I must make the most of time
  And drift not with the tide,
For killing time's not murder,
  It's more like suicide.

UNKNOWN

I never knew the old gentleman with the scythe and hourglass bring anything but grey hairs, thin cheeks, and loss of teeth.

DRYDEN

More haste, less speed.

AUGUSTUS CAESAR

That proverbial saying "Bad news travels fast and far."

PLUTARCH

War

For what avail the plow or sail
Or land or life, if freedom fail?

RALPH WALDO EMERSON

Then happy low, lie down!
Uneasy lies the head that wears a crown.

WILLIAM SHAKESPEARE

We join ourselves to no party that does not carry the flag and keep step to the music of the Union.

RUFUS CHOATE

If Europe should ever be ruined, it will be by its warriors.

BARON DE MONTESQUIEU

In all the trade of war, no feat
Is nobler than a brave retreat.

BUTLER

Give me the money that has been spent in war, and I will purchase every foot of land upon the globe. I will clothe every man, woman and child in an attire of which kings and queens would be proud. I will build a school house on every hillside, and in every valley over the whole earth; I will build an academy in every town, and endow it; a college in every State, and fill it with able professors; I will crown every hill with a place of worship, consecrated to the promulgation of the gospel of peace; I will support in every pulpit an able teacher of righteousness, so that on every Sabbath morning the chime on one hill should answer to the chime on another round the earth's wide circumference; and the voice of prayer, and the song of praise, should ascend like an universal holocaust to heaven.

HENRY RICHARD

It is better to have a lion at the head of an army of sheep, than a sheep at the head of an army of lions.

DEFOE

No wild enthusiast ever yet could rest
Till half mankind were like himself possessed.

WILLIAM COWPER

By gnawing through a dyke even a rat may drown a nation.

EDWARD BURKE

Forewarned forearmed.

MIGUEL DE CERVANTES

I came, I saw, I conquered.

JULIUS CAESAR

We make war that we can live in peace.

ARISTOTLE

Force has no place where there is need of skill.

HERODOTUS

Even in war, moral power is to physical as three parts out of four.

NAPOLEON I

There is one certain means by which I can be sure never to see my country's ruin—*I will die in the last ditch.*

WILLIAM III, PRINCE OF ORANGE

Wisdom

As the ancients
Say wisely, have a care o'th main chance,
And look before you ere you leap;
For as you sow, ye are like to reap.

SAMUEL BUTLER

No man can safely isolate himself, either intellectually or in practical matters.

A. MACLAREN, D.D.

He alone is an acute observer who can observe minutely without being observed.

JOHANN KASPAR LAVATER

He who reforms himself, has done more towards reforming the public, than a crowd of noisy, impotent patriots.

JOHANN KASPAR LAVATER

When pride begins, love ceases.

'Tis better that a man's own works, than that another man's words should praise him.

SIR ROGER L'ESTRANGE

Who makes quick use of the moment is a genius of prudence.

JOHANN KASPAR LAVATER

The wisest man is he who does not fancy that he is so at all.

NICOLAS BOILEAU-DESPREAUX

When a true genius appears in the world you may know him by this sign, that the dunces are all in confederacy against him.

JONATHAN SWIFT

WISDOM

Knowledge and wisdom, far from being
    one,
Have oft times no connection. Knowledge
    dwells
In heads replete with thoughts of other men:
Wisdom in minds attentive to their own.
Knowledge is proud that he has learned so
    much;
Wisdom is humble that he knows no more.

WILLIAM COWPER

No man is wise who is not good. No man is wise who is not humble.

UNKNOWN

A narrow mind begets obstinacy, and we do not easily believe what we cannot see.

JOHN DRYDEN

The best things are not bought and sold.

WALTER SMITH, D.D.

A fool says, "I can't"; a wise man says, "I'll try."

UNKNOWN

Learn as if you were to live for ever; live as if you were to die to-morrow.

UNKNOWN

A handful of common sense is worth a bushel of learning.

SPANISH PROVERB

If a man would register all his opinions upon love, politics, religion, and learning, what a bundle of inconsistencies and contradictions would appear at last!

JONATHAN SWIFT

It is quality rather than quantity that matters.

SENECA

A journey of a thousand miles must begin with a single step.

LAO TZU

TRUE

Refuse to open your purse, and soon you cannot open your sympathy. Refuse to give, and soon you will cease to enjoy that which you have. Refuse to love, and you lose the power to love and be loved. Withhold your affections and you become a moral paralytic. But the moment you open wider the door of your life, you let the sunshine of your life into some soul.

UNKNOWN

A promise should be made by the heart and remembered by the hand.

UNKNOWN

Brevity is the soul of wit.

WILLIAM SHAKESPEARE

No man can hold another man in the gutter without remaining there himself.

BOOKER T. WASHINGTON

When a man has not a good reason for doing a thing, he has one good reason for letting it alone.

SIR WALTER SCOTT

All's well that ends well; still the fine's the crown.

WILLIAM SHAKESPEARE

True eloquence consists in saying all that should be, not all that could be said.

DUC DE LA ROCHEFOUCAULD

Free and fair discussion will ever be found the firmest friend to truth.

GEORGE CAMPBELL

Everything has two handles; the one soft and manageable, the other such as will not endure to be touched. If then your brother do you an injury, do not take it by the hot hard handle, by representing to yourself all the aggravating circumstances of the fact; but look rather on the soft side, and extenuate it as much as is possible, by considering the nearness of the relation, and the long friendship and familiarity between you—obligations to kindness which a single provocation ought not to dissolve. And thus you will take the accident by its manageable handle.

EPICTETUS

Leave unsaid the wrong thing at the tempting moment.

UNKNOWN

Talking comes by nature, silence by wisdom.

UNKNOWN

If wisdom's ways you wisely seek, five
things observe with care:

Of whom you speak, to whom you speak,
and how, and when, and where.

UNKNOWN

Much learning does not teach a man to have intelligence.

HERACLITUS

The wise learn many things from their enemies

ARISTOPHANES

Go to the ant . . . consider her ways, and be wise!

SOLOMON

Ability wins us the esteem of the true men; luck that of the people.

DUC DE LA ROCHEFOUCAULD

There is nothing more beautiful in this world than a healthy wise old man.

LIN YUTANG

Make the most of the day, by determining to spend it on *two* sorts of acquaintances only— those by whom something may be got, and those from whom something may be learned.

CHARLES CALEB COLTON

Common sense in an uncommon degree is what the world calls wisdom.

COLERIDGE

Where ignorance is bliss
'Tis folly to be wise.

THOMAS GRAY

Death and life are in the power of the tongue.

SOLOMON

What shall it profit a man, if he gain the whole world and lose his own soul?

JESUS CHRIST

Testimony is like an arrow shot from a long bow; the force of it depends on the strength of the hand that draws it. Argument is like an arrow from a cross-bow, which has equal force though shot by a child.

BACON

I am not mad; I would to heaven I were!
For then, 'tis like I should forget myself;
O, if I could, what grief should I forget!

WILLIAM SHAKESPEARE

Four things belong to a judge; to hear courteously, to answer wisely, to consider soberly, and to decide impartially.

SOCRATES

There are two sides to every question.

PROTAGORAS

Encouragement is oxygen to the soul! No one ever climbed spiritual heights without it. No one ever lived without it.

UNKNOWN

*Once to every man and nation comes the
    moment to decide;
In the strife of Truth and Falsehood, for the
    good or evil side;
Some great cause, God's new Messiah,
    offering each the bloom or blight,
Parts the goats upon the left hand and the
    sheep upon the right,
And the choice goes by forever 'twixt that
    darkness and that light.*

JAMES RUSSELL LOWELL

Liberty consists in the power of doing that which is permitted by law.

CICERO

What is justice? To give every man his due.

ARISTOTLE

The censure of those that are opposed to us, is the nicest commendation that can be given us.

ST. EVREMOND

*My endeavors
Have ever come too short of my desire.*

WILLIAM SHAKESPEARE

What too many orators want in depth, they give you in length.

BARON DE MONTESQUIEU

What's in a name? That which we call
    a rose
By any other name would smell as sweet.

WILLIAM SHAKESPEARE

Opinion, that great fool, makes fools of all.

FIELD

Justice is lame as well as blind among us.

THOMAS OTWAY

Philosophy, when superficially studied, excites doubt; when thoroughly explored, it dispels it.

FRANCIS BACON

He who reigns within himself, and rules passions, desires and fears, is more than a king.

JOHN MILTON

If you would be pungent, be brief; for it is with words as with sunbeams—the more they are condensed the deeper they burn.

ROBERT SOUTHEY

They are never alone that are accompanied with noble thoughts.

SIR PHILIP SIDNEY

He that uses many words for the explaining any subject, doth, like the cuttlefish, hide himself for the most part in his own ink.

JOHN RAY

The difference between perseverance and obstinancy is that one often comes from a strong will, and the other from a strong won't.

HENRY WARD BEECHER

Slow and steady wins the race.

AESOP

Let us cling to our principles as the mariner clings to his last plank when night and tempest close around him.

ANON.

Union gives strength.

AESOP

OPPORTUNITY

When one door closes, another opens; but we often look so long and so regretfully upon the closed door that we do not see the one which has opened for us.

ALEXANDER GRAHAM BELL

There is no riches above a sound body, and no joy above the joy of the heart.

ECCLESIASTICUS

He may hope for the best that's prepared for the worst.

UNKNOWN

A rolling stone gathers no moss.

PUBLIUS SYRUS

Temper is so good a thing that we should never lose it.

UNKNOWN

It is sometimes necessary to play the fool to avoid being deceived by cunning men.

DUC DE LA ROCHEFOUCAULD

Early to bed and early to rise, makes a man healthy, wealthy, and wise.

BENJAMIN FRANKLIN

Two heads are better than one.

JOHN HEYWOOD

Giving advice to a fool is like giving medicine to a dead man.

AMERICAN SAYING

Meddle with dirt and some of it will stick to you.

UNKNOWN

To scare a bird is not the way to catch it.

UNKNOWN

The best is the cheapest in the end.

UNKNOWN

A promise is a debt that we may not forget.

UNKNOWN

The best sort of revenge is not to be like him who did the injury.

MARCUS AURELIUS ANTONINUS

He who purposes to be an author should first be a student.

JOHN DRYDEN

Better to be despised for too anxious apprehensions, than ruined by too confident a security.

EDMUND BURKE

Hasty judgments are generally faulty ones.

UNKNOWN

Persuasion is better than force.

UNKNOWN

A good education is the best dowry.

UNKNOWN

A little oil may save a deal of friction.

UNKNOWN

Waste makes want.

UNKNOWN

As you make your bed, so you must lie on it.

UNKNOWN

A good example is the best sermon.

UNKNOWN

Things are not always what they seem.

PHAEDRUS

A lean compromise is better than a fat lawsuit.

UNKNOWN

Discretion in speech is more than eloquence.

FRANCIS BACON

O wad some pow'r the giftie gie us
To see oursels as others see us!

It wad frae mony a blunder free us,
  And foolish notion.

ROBERT BURNS

Alternate rest and labor long endure.

OVID

And now abideth faith, hope, and charity,
these three; but the greatest of these is charity.

1 COR. XIII, 13

An extraordinary haste to discharge an
obligation is a sort of ingratitude.

DUC DE LA ROCHEFOUCAULD

Better not be at all,
Than not be noble.

ALFRED, LORD TENNYSON

He who is most slow in making a promise, is
the most faithful in the performance of it.

JEAN JACQUES ROUSSEAU

The future is a great land . . . It is wider than
the vision and has no end.

UNKNOWN

Our doubts are traitors,
And make us lose the good we oft

might *win,*
By. *fearing to attempt.*

WILLIAM SHAKESPEARE

By work you get money, by talk you get knowledge.

THOMAS CHANDLER HALIBURTON

LETTERS

Letters are a silken thread
That runs from heart to heart,
Weaving a web of things unsaid
When we must be apart.

UNKNOWN

Wise men learn by other men's mistakes, fools by their own.

UNKNOWN

He who knows little, soon repeats it.

SPANISH PROVERB

All men desire by nature to know.

ARISTOTLE

Cleverness is as dexterity of the fingers— only of worth when under the control of kindness and wisdom.

THOMAS LYNCH

Wisdom in the man, patience in the wife,
bring peace to the house, and a happy life.

UNKNOWN

Genius is the highest type of reason—talent
the highest type of the understanding.

HICKOK

Wisdom is rare.

UNKNOWN

INSIGHT

Often when it seemed I found
Goodness here, there, all around,
I saw on closer scrutiny,
The goodness came from inside me.

Why did the whole world seem to smile?
Because I laughed with it awhile.
Why was all earth so bright with sun?
Because my light heart gave it one.

What made the future seem so bright,
The past seem dear, the future right?
What was it set the day apart?
The peace of God within my heart.
Since then when life looks dark and grim,
My assets small, my prospects dim,
I push dark thoughts back on the shelf,
And seek for heaven in myself.

UNKNOWN

Wealth may seek us; but wisdom must be sought.

UNKNOWN

It is far easier to be wise for others than to be so for oneself.

DUC DE LA ROCHEFOUCAULD

All human wisdom is summed up in two words—wait and hope.

ALEXANDRE DUMAS

Few persons have sufficient wisdom to prefer censure which is useful to them, to praise which deceives them.

DUC DE LA ROCHEFOUCAULD

The precious porcelain of common clay.

LORD BYRON

The debt immense of endless gratitude.

JOHN MILTON

That only can with propriety be styled refinement which by strengthening the intellect, purifies the manners.

SAMUEL TAYLOR COLERIDGE

The three indispensables of genius are understanding, feeling, and perseverance. The three things that enrich genius are contentment of mind, the cherishing of good thoughts, and exercising the memory.

ROBERT SOUTHEY

A sentence well couched takes both the sense and the understanding. I love not those cart-rope speeches that are longer than the memory of man can fathom.

OWEN FELTHAM

It is a special trick of low cunning to squeeze out knowledge from a modest man, who is eminent in any science, and then to use it as legally acquired, and pass the source in total silence.

HORACE WALPOLE

A college education shows a man how little other people know.

THOMAS CHANDLER HALIBURTON

It is impossible to make people understand their ignorance, for it requires knowledge to perceive it; and, therefore, he that can perceive it hath it not.

JEREMY TAYLOR

Half the world knows not how the other half lives.

GEORGE HERBERT

It is better to have nothing to do, then to be doing nothing.

ATTICUS

Facts are to the mind the same thing as food to the body. On the due digestion of facts depends the strength and wisdom of the one, just as vigor and health depend on the other. The wisest in council, the ablest in debate, and the most agreeable in the commerce of life, is that man who has assimilated to his understanding the greatest number of facts.

BURKE

'Tis education forms the common mind:
Just as the twig is bent, the tree's inclin'd.

ALEXANDER POPE

No sense so uncommon as common sense.

UNKNOWN

Examinations are formidable even to the best prepared, for the greatest fool may ask more than the wisest man can answer.

CHARLES CALEB COLTON

A little learning is a dangerous thing.

ALEXANDER POPE

The first step to knowledge is to know that we are ignorant.

RICHARD CECIL

Knowledge is power.

FRANCIS BACON

The veil which covers the face of futurity is woven by the hand of mercy.

EDWARD GEORGE BULWER-LYTTON

There is one art of which every man should be a master—the art of reflection.

SAMUEL TAYLOR COLERIDGE

In politics, what begins in fear usually ends in folly.

COLERIDGE

Errors like straws upon the surface flow:
He who would search for pearls must dive
below.

JOHN DRYDEN

Superstition renders a man a fool, and scepticism makes him mad.

HENRY FIELDING

A bitter jest, when the satire comes too near the truth, leaves a sharp sting behind.

TACITUS

No life can be dreary when work is delight.

FRANCIS RIDLEY HAVERGAL

Ill ware is never cheap. Pleasing ware is half sold.

GEORGE HERBERT

They condemn what they do not understand.

CICERO

Convention is the ruler of all.

PINDAR

We sow a thought and reap an act,
  We sow an act and reap a habit,
We sow a habit and reap a character,
  We sow a character and reap a destiny.

WILLIAM MAKEPEACE THACKERY

Grief divided is made lighter.

UNKNOWN

Woman

Who can find a virtuous woman?
  her price is far above rubies.
The heart of her husband doth safely trust
  in her, so that he shall have no need
  of spoil.
She will do him good and not evil all the
  days of her life.
She seeketh wool and flax, and worketh
  willingly with her hands.
She is like the merchants' ships; she
  bringeth her food from afar.
She riseth also while it is yet night, and
  giveth meat to her household, and a
  portion to her maidens.
She considereth a field, and buyeth it; with
  the fruit of her hands she planteth a
  vineyard.

She girdeth her loins with strength, and
  strengtheneth her arms.
She perceiveth that her merchandise is good;
  her candle goeth not out by night.
She layeth her hands to the spindle, and
  her hands hold the distaff.
She stretcheth out her hand to the poor;
  yea, she reacheth forth her hands to
  the needy.
She is not afraid of the snow for her
  household: for all her household are
  clothed with scarlet.
She maketh herself coverings of tapestry;
  her clothing is silk and purple.
Her husband is known in the gates, when he
  sitteth among the elders of the land.
She maketh fine linen, and selleth it; and
  delivereth girdles unto the merchant.
Strength and honor are her clothing; and
  she shall rejoice in time to come.
She openeth her mouth with wisdom; and in
  her tongue is the law of kindness.
She looketh well to the ways of her
  household, and eateth not the bread of
  idleness.
Her children arise up, and call her blessed;
  her husband also, and he praiseth her.
Many daughters have done virtuously, but
  thou excellest them all.
Favor is deceitful, and beauty is vain: but
  a woman that feareth the Lord, she
  shall be praised.
Give her of the fruit of her hands; and let
  her own works praise her in the gates.

PROVERBS

Blessed is the man that hath a virtuous wife,
for the number of his days shall be double.

ECCLESIASTICUS

He's a fool, who thinks by force, or skill,
To turn the current of a woman's will.

SAMUEL TUKE

Women have more strength in their looks
than we have in our laws, and more power in
their tears than we have by our arguments.

SAVILLE

Disguise our bondage as we will,
'Tis woman, woman rules us still.

THOMAS MOORE

A world of comfort lies in that one word,
wife.

KNOWLES

What is there in the vale of life
Half so delightful as a wife;
When friendship, love, and peace combine
To stamp the marriage-bond divine?

WILLIAM COWPER

They talk about a woman's sphere,
  As though it had a limit;
There's not a place in earth or heaven,
There's not a task to mankind given,
There's not a blessing or a woe,
There's not a whisper, Yes or No,
There's not a life, or death, or birth,
That has a feather's weight of worth,
  Without a woman in it.

UNKNOWN

The lady doth protest too much, methinks.

WILLIAM SHAKESPEARE

When the candles are out all women are fair.

PLUTARCH

O men, respect women who have borne you.

THE KORAN

These impossible women! How they do get
    around us!
The poet was right; can't live with them, or
    without them!

ARISTOPHANES

She who ne'er answers till a husband
    cools,
Or, if she rules him, never shows she rules;
Charms by accepting, by submitting, sways,
Yet has her humor most, when she obeys.

ALEXANDER POPE

Her voice was ever soft,
Gentle, and low; an excellent thing in
    woman.

WILLIAM SHAKESPEARE

All other goods by Fortune's hand are
    given,
A wife is the peculiar gift of heaven.

POPE

O Woman! in our hours of ease,
Uncertain, coy, and hard to please,
And variable as the shade
By the light quivering aspen made;
When pain and anguish wring the brow
A ministering angel thou!

SIR WALTER SCOTT

Men have many faults;
  Poor women have but two;
There's nothing good they say,
  And nothing right they do.

ANON.

Would'st thou clearly learn what true nobili-
ty is? Inquire of noble-minded women.

GERMAN SAYING

A cheerful wife is the joy of life.

UNKNOWN

A good wife and health are a man's best
wealth.

UNKNOWN

A woman's idea of a square deal is one in
which she comes out ahead.

UNKNOWN

Men make houses, but women make homes.

UNKNOWN

I believe that marriage should be a perfect partnership; that a woman should have all the rights that a man has, and one more—the right to be protected. I do not like the man who thinks he is boss. The fellow in the dugout was always talking about being boss. I do not like a man who thinks he has got authority and that the woman belongs to him—that wants his wife for a slave. I would not want the love of a woman that is not great enough, grand enough, and splendid enough to be free. I will never give to any woman my heart upon whom I afterwards put chains.

ROBERT GREEN INGERSOLL

What manly eloquence could produce such an effect as woman's silence.

JULES MICHELET

Woman's natural mission is to love, to love but one, to love always.

JULES MICHELET

SOMEBODY'S MOTHER

The woman was old, and ragged and gray.
And bent with the chill of the winter's day.
The street was wet with the recent snow,
And the woman's feet were aged and slow.

She stood at the crossing and waited long
Alone, uncared for, amid the throng
Of human beings who passed her by,
Nor heeded the glance of her anxious eye.

Down the street with laughter and shout,
Glad in the freedom of "school let out,"
Came the boys like a flock of sheep,
Hailing the snow piled white and deep.

Past the woman so old and gray,
Hastened the children on their way,
Nor offered a helping hand to her,
So meek, so timid, afraid to stir,
Lest the carriage wheels or the horses feet
Should crowd her down in the slippery
     street.

At last came one of the merry troop,
The gayest laddie of all the group;
He paused beside her and whispered low,
"I'll help you across if you wish to go."

Her aged hand on his strong young arm
She placed, and so, without hurt or harm,
He guided her trembling feet along,
Proud that his own were firm and strong.

Then back again to his friends he went,
His young heart happy and well content.
"She's somebody's mother, boys, you know,
For all she's aged and poor and slow;

"And I hope some fellow will lend a hand
To help my mother, you understand,
If ever she's poor, and old, and gray,
When her own dear boy is far away."

And "somebody's mother" bowed low her
     head,
In her home that night, and the prayer
     she said,
Was, "God be kind to the noble boy,
Who is somebody's son and pride and joy."

UNKNOWN

Woman's happiness is in obeying. She objects to men who abdicate too much.

JULES MICHELET

Woman knows that the better she obeys the surer she is to rule.

JULES MICHELET

MOTHER'S WRINKLED HANDS

Such beautiful, beautiful hands!
Though heart were weary and sad
Those patient hands kept toiling on
That her children might be glad.
I almost weep when looking back
To childhood's distant day!
I think how these hands rested not
When mine were at their play.

UNKNOWN

A WOMAN'S QUESTION

Do you know you have asked for the
    costliest thing
  Ever made by the hand above?
A woman's heart, and a woman's life—
  And a woman's wonderful love.

Do you know you have asked for this
    priceless thing
  As a child might ask for a toy?
Demanding what others have died to win,
  With the reckless dash of a boy.

You have written my lesson of duty out;
  Manlike, you have questioned me.
Now stand at the bar of my woman's soul
  Until I shall question thee.

You require your mutton shall be always
  hot,

Your socks and your shirts be whole;
I require your heart to be true as God's
    stars
  And as pure as His heaven your soul.

You require a cook for your mutton and
    beef;
  I require a far greater thing;
A seamstress you're wanting for socks and
    shirts—
  I look for a man and a king.

A king for the beautiful realm called Home,
  And a man that his maker, God,
Shall look upon as He did on the first
  And say "It is very good."

I require all things that are grand and true,
  All things that a man should be;
If you give this all, I would stake my life
  To be all you demand of me.

Is your heart an ocean so strong and deep,
  I may launch my all on its tide?
A loving woman finds heaven or hell
  On the day she is made a bride.

I am fair and young, but the rose may fade
  From my soft young cheek one day;
Will you love me then 'mid the falling
    leaves,
  As you did 'mong the blossoms of May?

If you cannot be this, a laundress and cook
  You can hire and little to pay;
But a woman's heart and a woman's life
  Are not to be won that way.

                              LENA LATHROP

She neglects her heart who studies her glass.

JOHANN KASPAR LAVATER

She looketh as butter would not melt in her mouth.

JOHN HEYWOOD